AN ORIGINAL HO'

CW01677870

COMPLETE USER'S GUIDE

Canon EOS 300 EOS Rebel 2000

BY PHILIP RABY

HOVE FOTO BOOKS

Canon EOS 300
EOS Rebel 2000

All text, illustrations and data apply to cameras with either name.

First English Edition Hove Foto Books Nov 1999

Newpro UK Limited
Old Sawmills Road, Faringdon, Oxon.
SN7 7DS, England
Tel: (01367) 242411 Fax: (01367) 241124

Typeset and produced by William J Anthony Partnership Limited
Newlands Building, Lowlands, Vale, Guernsey, Channel Islands GY3 5XJ

Printed by
Wincanton Press Co. Ltd., Great Britain

British Library Cataloguing-in-Publication Data
A catalogue record for this book is available from the British Library

Philip Raby

ISBN : 1-874031-32-0

Worldwide Distribution:

Newpro UK Ltd.,
Old Sawmills Road, Faringdon, Oxon.,
SN7 7DS, England
Tel: (01367) 242411 Fax: (01367) 241124

Contents

Chapter 1

Introduction

A brief history of Canon

Congratulations on buying a Canon EOS 300 – Rebel 2000. You have bought a camera with an enviable heritage. The origins of Canon date back to the 1930s, when two Japanese entrepreneurs decided to build a 35mm rangefinder camera that would compete with the finest European models.

Their first prototypes were called Kwannons, of which there is only one surviving example. The brand was named after a Buddhist deity, but was changed to Canon in 1935 to avoid offending religious groups and to be more appealing to western buyers. The two names are pronounced identically in Japan.

The early Canons were rangefinder models and owed their styling to the popular Leica models of the day. The first Canon SLR camera was introduced in 1959. SLR stands for Single Lens Reflex and means that the viewfinder image is formed from light passing through the lens, so what you see in the viewfinder is the image that forms on the film during exposure. Your EOS 300 – Rebel 2000 is an SLR design.

A series of Canon SLR cameras was produced during the 1950s and 1960s. In the 1970s, Canon started to produce cameras that used electronics to control the exposure and shutter system. This was a revolution that led to the world beating AE-1 of 1976. This remarkable camera was an instant hit and became a best-seller. It was followed by the even more successful A-1, which introduced many features now found in your EOS 300 – Rebel 2000, such as Shutter Priority, Aperture Priority and Program modes, and a LED viewfinder read-out that let you see the set shutter speed and aperture without taking your eye away from the camera.

These features were later incorporated into the futuristic – and now classic – Canon T90, which turned camera design upside down with its smooth, ergonomic curves.

The T90 led the way for the first EOS – the EOS 650. Introduced in 1987, this camera was a gamble for Canon because it used a totally new lens mount system that was not compatible with earlier Canon cameras and lenses. The reason for the new mount was that the camera featured a revolutionary autofocus system that relied on a focus motor in the lens. Other manufacturers were developing autofocus cameras with motors in the body, but Canon's engineers decided that this was a compromise and would not give the fast, accurate focusing that top photographers demanded.

Canon's gamble paid off. There have now been over 20 EOS models and they have become the most popular SLR cameras in the world.

By the way, in case you're wondering, EOS stands for Electro Optical System. And Eos was the Greek goddess of dawn, daughter of Helios and mother of Memnon. So now you know!

The EOS 300 – Rebel 2000 was launched in 1999. It is a superb entry-level EOS camera that replaces the extremely popular EOS 500N, known as the EOS Rebel G in North America.

What this book will do for you

This book is a detailed guide to the EOS 300 – Rebel 2000 and its accessories, it is not a general guide to photography. However, when read in conjunction with the camera instruction book, it will help you to understand fully the operation of this wonderful little camera. In turn, that will enable you to take better photographs.

Model names

In North America the EOS 300 is known as the EOS Rebel 2000. Throughout the book the North American name is given after the international name.

Quartz Date (QD) versions of the cameras are available. Except where specifically referred to, these cameras are identical to the non-QD versions.

Chapter 2

Finding your way around

The EOS 300 – Rebel 2000 is designed to be simple and straightforward to use. However, to get the very best from your camera you should get to know it so well that it becomes an extension of your hands – nothing should come between you and your photography – not even a camera!

The best way to learn the camera's controls is to use them, but you can give yourself a head start by reading this chapter and trying out all the features in the comfort of your home.

Each camera feature is briefly described and, where relevant, includes a chapter reference (see diagram 1 and 2).

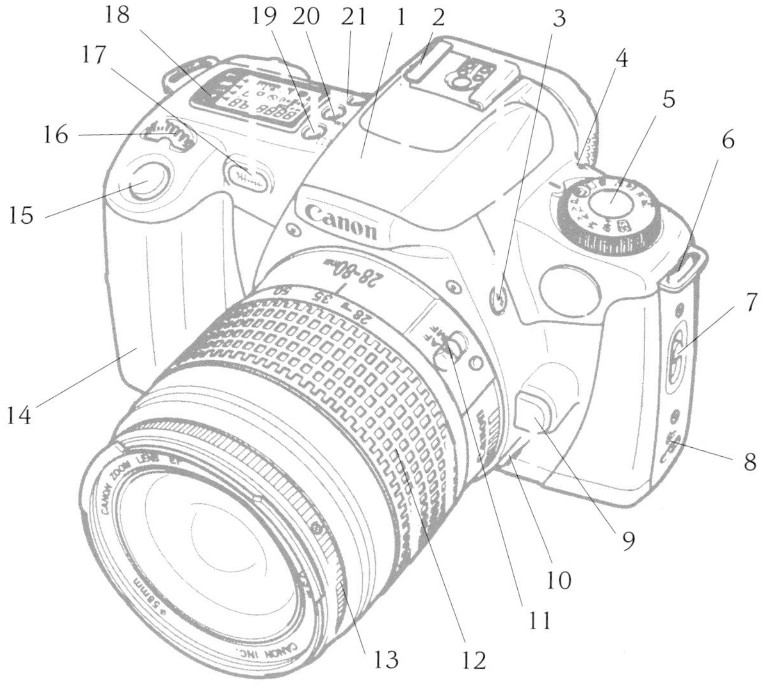

Diagram 1

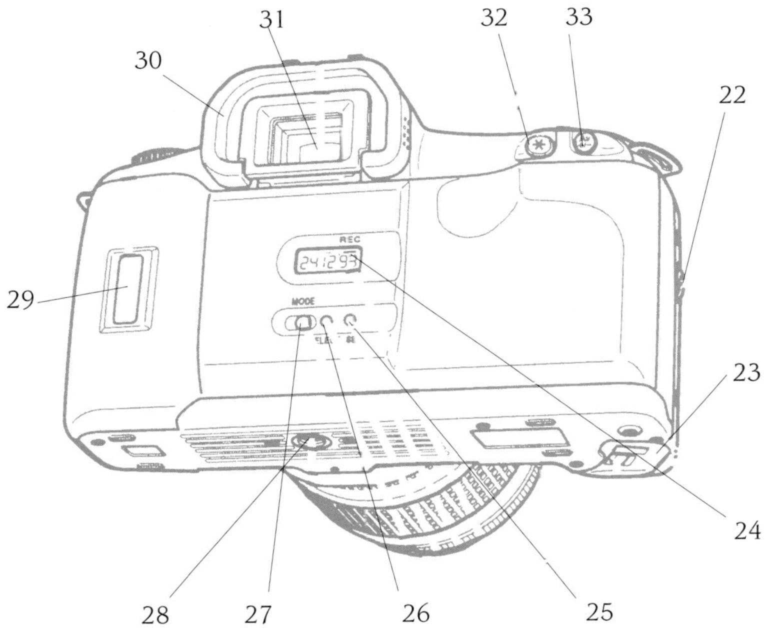

Diagram 2

1. Built-in flash

The EOS 300 – Rebel 2000 has a handy built-in flash unit. This pops up automatically when required in Full-Auto and some PIC modes. In Creative Zone modes, it can be activated manually when required by pressing the Flash button.

Chapter 12, 13

2. Hotshoe

This allows a dedicated Speedlite flashgun to be attached to the camera. The hotshoe has a number of electrical contacts that allow the camera and Speedlite to communicate with each other during TTL, A-TTL and E-TTL flash photography.

The hotshoe also accepts other accessories, including an off-camera flash lead, remote control receptor or a hotshoe/PC adaptor for connecting the camera to studio flash units. Another handy accessory that fits onto the hotshoe is a mini spirit level (available from photo dealers) for checking that the camera is horizontal.

Chapter 12, 13, 14

3. Flash button

Press this button to activate the built-in flash in Creative Zone modes.

Chapter 12, 13

4. Film plane mark

Indicates the position of the film plane – useful only for measuring subject-to-film distances during extreme close-up photography.

5. Command Dial

A major control on the camera and a trademark feature that makes EOS cameras so easy to use.

The Command Dial is used to set the shooting mode – choose from Full Auto, five PIC modes and five Creative Zone modes.

When you are not using your camera, turn the Command Dial to 'L'. This is the Lock position that turns off the camera and prevents the shutter button being depressed accidentally.

6. Neck strap lug

There is one of these on each end of the camera for attaching a neck strap. Carrying your camera on a strap around your neck ensures that it is always ready for action and safe from being dropped.

Chapter 3

7. Camera back latch

Slide this latch downwards to open the camera back for loading and unloading film. Before doing so, look through the film window to see if a film is loaded. If there is, check the LCD panel to make sure the film symbol is flashing – this tells you that the film is fully rewound ready for removal. Never operate this catch when you are part-way through a film – the exposed frames will be fogged and you will lose your precious images.

Chapter 3

8. Midroll film rewind button

If you wish to remove a film part-way through, press this button to activate midroll rewind. It is recessed so that you cannot press it by accident.

Chapter 10

9. Lens Release button

This button must be pressed before the lens can be removed from the camera.

Chapter 3

10. Depth-of-field Preview button

Press this to stop the lens down by the preset amount to see the effect of aperture on depth-of-field.

11. Focus mode switch

This switch is found on most Canon EF lenses. When it is set to 'AF', autofocus is activated. Slide it to 'M' for manual focusing.

12. Zoom ring

Only found on Canon EF zoom lenses, turn this ring to set the lens focal length to suit the subject.

13. Focusing ring

Found on some Canon EF lenses, this ring is used for focusing when the Focus mode switch is set to 'M'. If your lens does not have a focusing ring, you have to turn the end of the lens barrel to focus manually.

14. Hand grip

Not only does this grip make the EOS 300 – Rebel 2000 easy and comfortable to hold, it also houses the lithium batteries that power the camera.

Chapter 3

15. Shutter release button

No camera would be complete without a shutter button. The one on your EOS 300 – Rebel 2000 has two steps. Press it half-way to activate autofocus and exposure metering. Press it all the way to fire the shutter and advance the film onto the next frame. It is not possible to use the shutter button when the Command Dial is set to Lock (L) or when the lens is unable to focus in One Shot mode.

When the shutter button is pressed halfway, the viewfinder display and LCD panel are activated. The display remains on for four seconds after releasing the shutter button.

To avoid camera shake spoiling your photographs, press the shutter button firmly but gently, taking care not to shake the camera.

16. Input Dial

This simple-to-use dial is operated by your right-hand index finger. Depending on the shooting mode the camera is in, the Input Dial is used to set the shutter speed, aperture, control Program Shift and much more. It turns in both directions and the settings made appear in the LCD panel and viewfinder display.

17. Self-timer and Red-eye Reduction lamp

During Self-timer operation, this light flashes twice a second for the first eight seconds of the countdown, and then increases in speed to eight flashes a second for the last two seconds before the shutter fires.

When Red-eye Reduction is activated, the lamp shines at the subject to make their retinas contract before taking a picture. This reduces the risk of red-eye occurring.

Chapter 15 and 13

18. LCD panel

This small panel displays a wealth of information about camera settings. See the diagram on page 17 for a full description. LCD stands for Liquid Crystal Display. After many years of use it is possible that the panel will fade and become hard to read. If this happens, return the camera to a Canon Authorised Service Centre to have the LCD panel replaced.

19. Focus point Selector button

This button allows you to manually choose the active focus point. Chapter 9

20. Function button

This button is used for a range of camera functions. Each time you press it a different function becomes active and is displayed in the LCD panel.

21. Self-timer button

This button activates the self-timer which delays the shutter firing for ten seconds after pressing the shutter button – ideal for self portraits, and for avoiding camera shake during long exposures.

Chapter 15

22. Remote Control socket

The EOS 300 – Rebel 2000 can be fitted with a remote control shutter release to avoid camera shake during long exposures and to fire the camera from a distance. This 2.5mm jack socket accepts the Canon Remote Switch RS60E3.

Chapter 18

23. Battery Compartment cover

Open this cover to insert the two CR2 batteries that are required to power the camera. Don't forget to always carry spare batteries in case the ones in the camera run down.

Chapter 3

24. Quartz Date display panel

Only found on QD version of the camera. Displays the currently set data.

Chapter 16

25. Quartz Date Set button

Only found on QD version of the camera. Is used to set the date functions

Chapter 16

26. Quartz Date Selection button

Only found on QD version of the camera. Is used to set the date functions

Chapter 16

27. Quartz Date Mode button

Only found on QD version of the camera. Is used to set the date functions

Chapter 16

28. Tripod socket

Accepts a standard tripod or monopod screw.

29. Film window

This handy feature lets you see at a glance whether or not a film is loaded in your camera. What's more, film manufacturers make sure that the essential information about film (type, speed, length) is printed on its cassette in such a position that it can be read through this window. Get into the habit of looking in here before you open the camera back.

Chapter 3

30. Viewfinder eyecup

This removable rubber surround provides a soft surface for your eye to rest against and blocks stray light from entering the viewfinder.

31. Viewfinder eyepiece

Look through here to see what you are taking a photograph of. If your eyesight is not perfect, you can fit a dioptre correction lens over the eyepiece to give a sharp image.

32. AE Lock button

Press this button to set AE Lock and Partial metering in Creative Zone modes.

Chapter 7

33. Exposure Compensation button

Press this button to set Exposure Compensation. Also used to set the aperture in Manual mode

Chapter 8

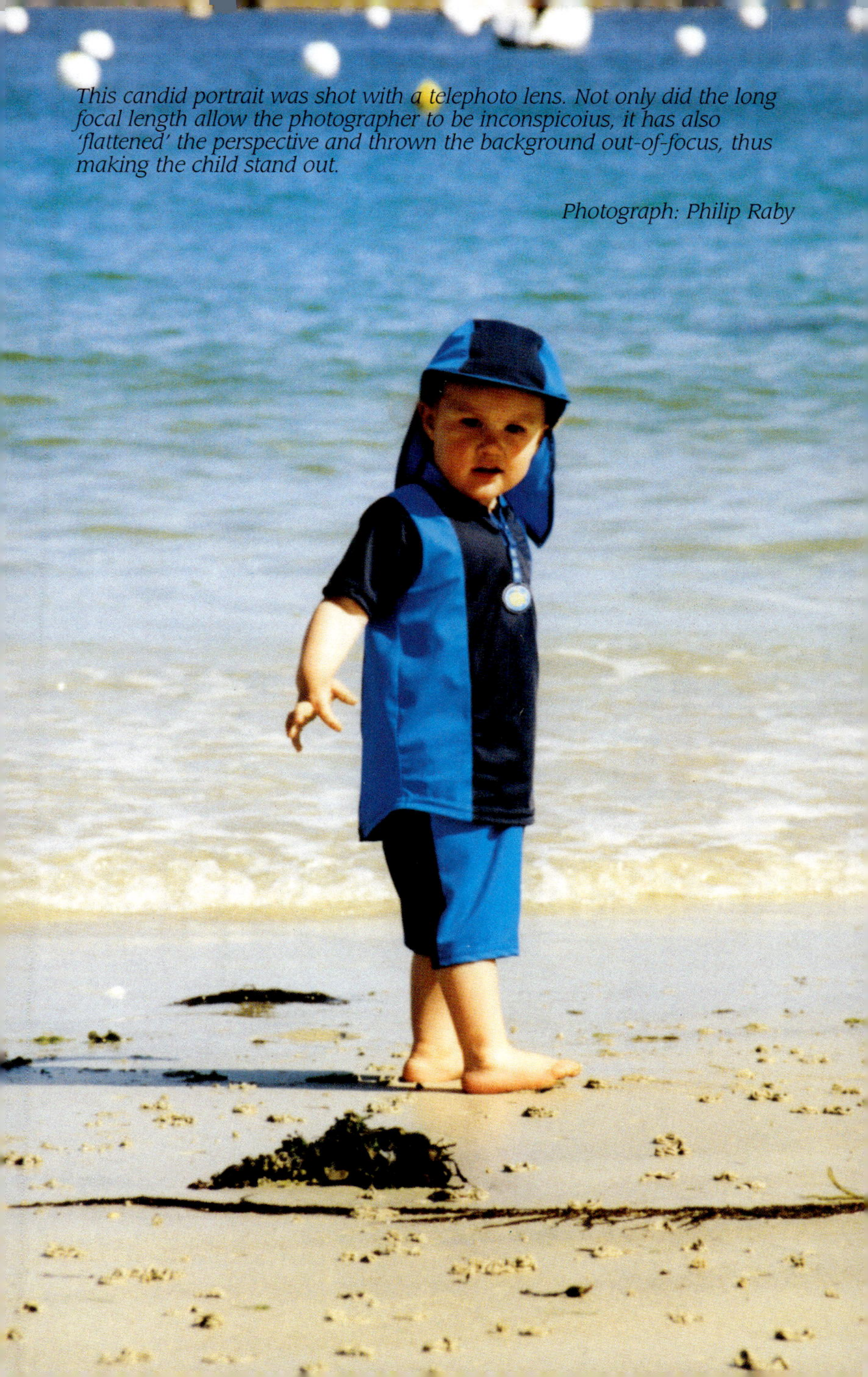

This candid portrait was shot with a telephoto lens. Not only did the long focal length allow the photographer to be inconspicoius, it has also 'flattened' the perspective and thrown the background out-of-focus, thus making the child stand out.

Photograph: Philip Raby

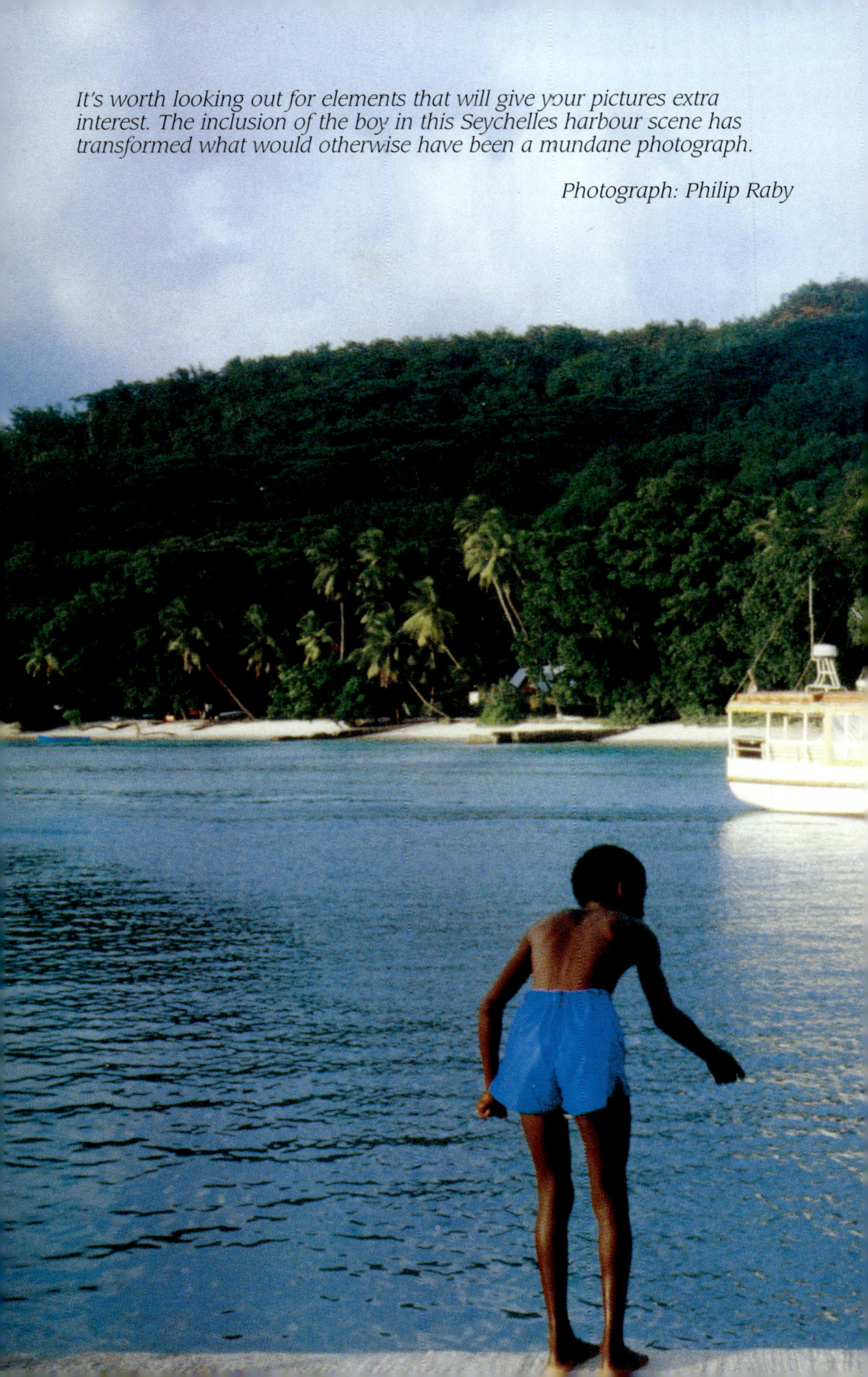

It's worth looking out for elements that will give your pictures extra interest. The inclusion of the boy in this Seychelles harbour scene has transformed what would otherwise have been a mundane photograph.

Photograph: Philip Raby

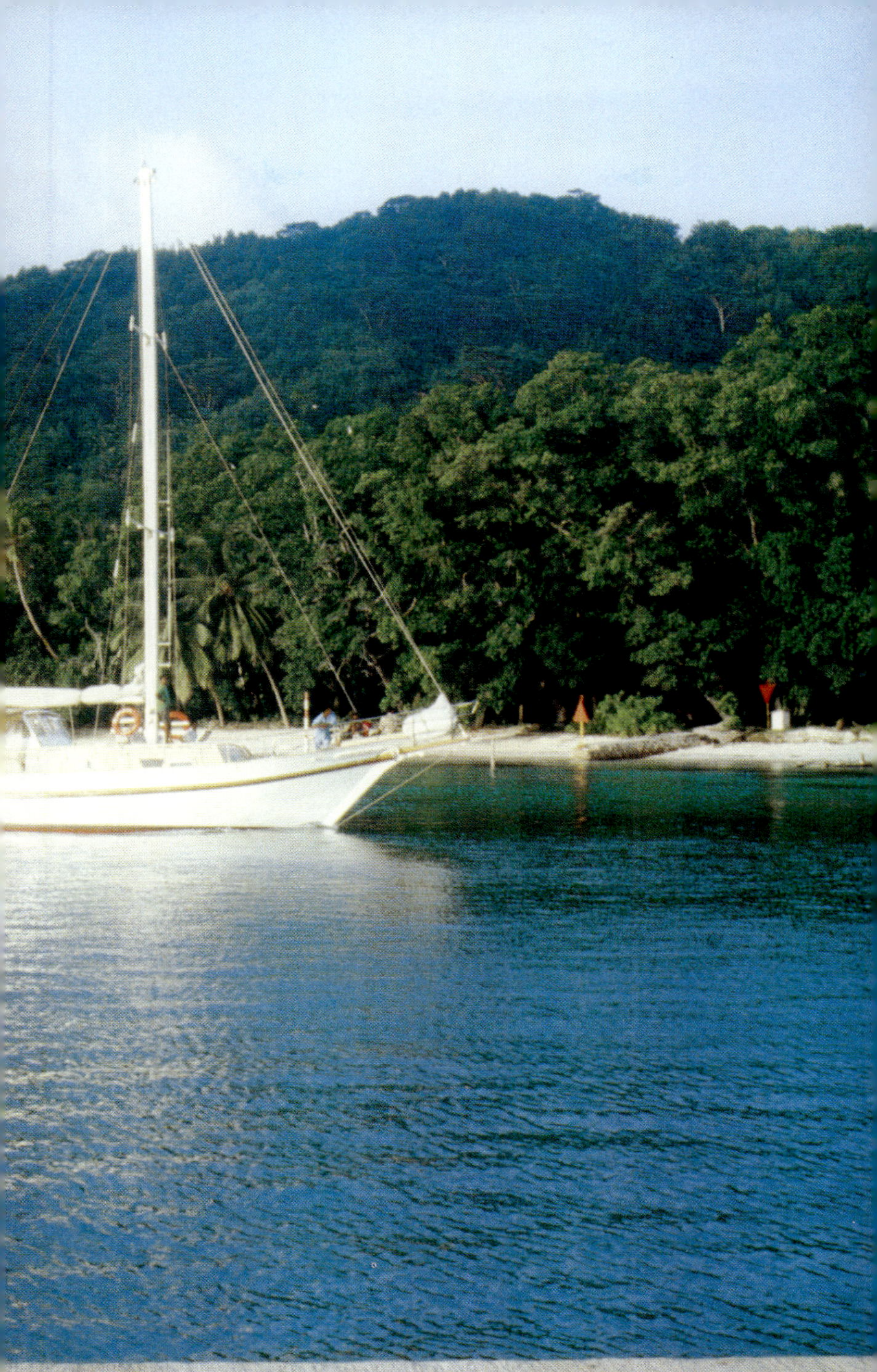

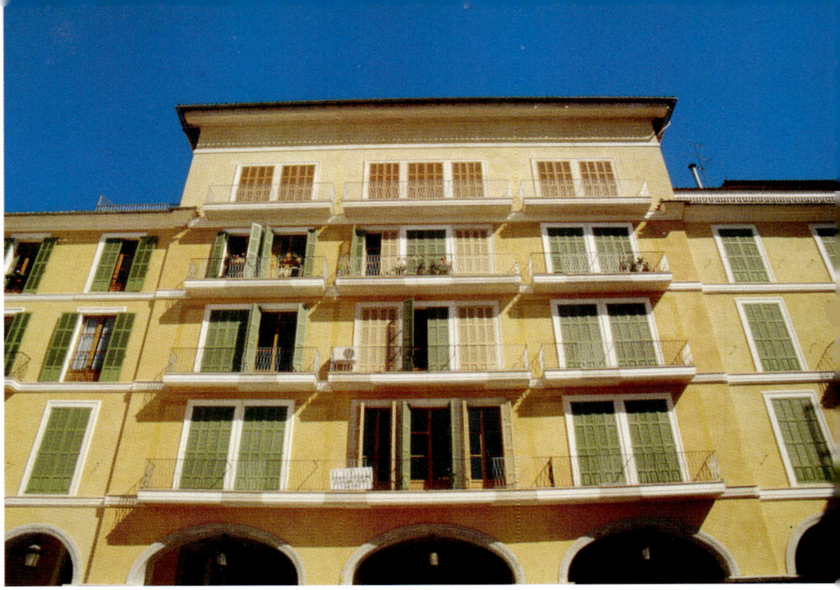

Both these photographs were taken with a standard zoom lens, and yet appear quite different. The first [[PIC 2]] was taken at the wide-angle setting so the photographer had to tip the camera up to include the top of the building in the photograph. This has led to so-called converging verticals. By moving away and using the telephoto setting, the photographer has been able to keep the camera back upright and thus avoiding converging verticals in the second version [[PIC 3]].

Photograph: Philip Raby

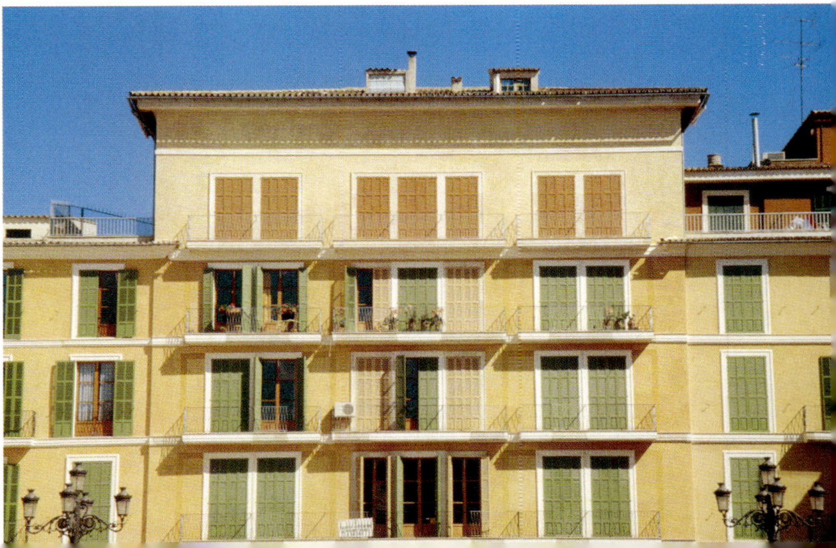

LCD panel

Diagram 3 shows all the information that can be displayed on the LCD panel. You'll never see all the symbols at one time, but it is a good idea to learn what they all mean.

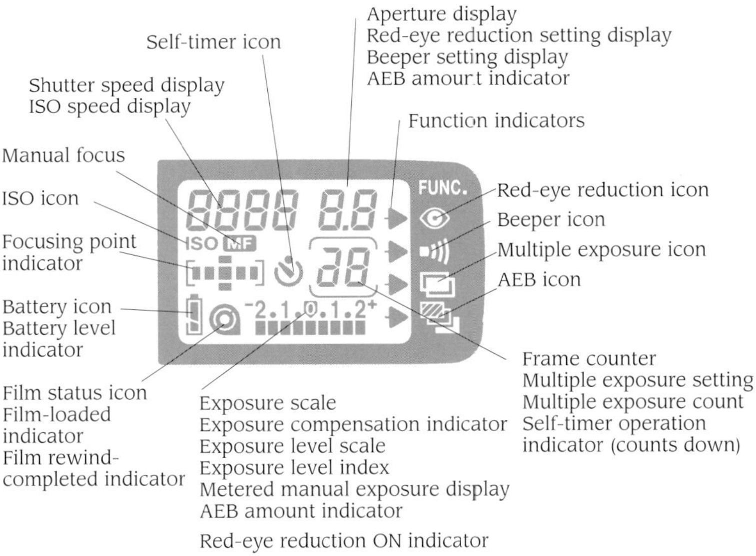

Diagram 3

The viewfinder

When you look into the viewfinder of the EOS 300 – Rebel 2000, this is what you see (diagram 4). When you half press the shutter button, the display at the bottom of the viewfinder comes on. It remains active for four seconds after the shutter button is released. If the shutter speed reading is blinking, it means that there is not enough light for hand-held photography without the risk of camera shake spoiling the photograph. Mount the camera on a tripod, monopod or other firm surface, or use flash. Your EOS 300 – Rebel 2000 uses the rule-of-thumb that says that the shutter speed should be at least 1/focal length for hand-held photography. Therefore, if you are using a short focal length lens, such as 28mm, you can get away with longer shutter speeds than when you are using a telephoto lens.

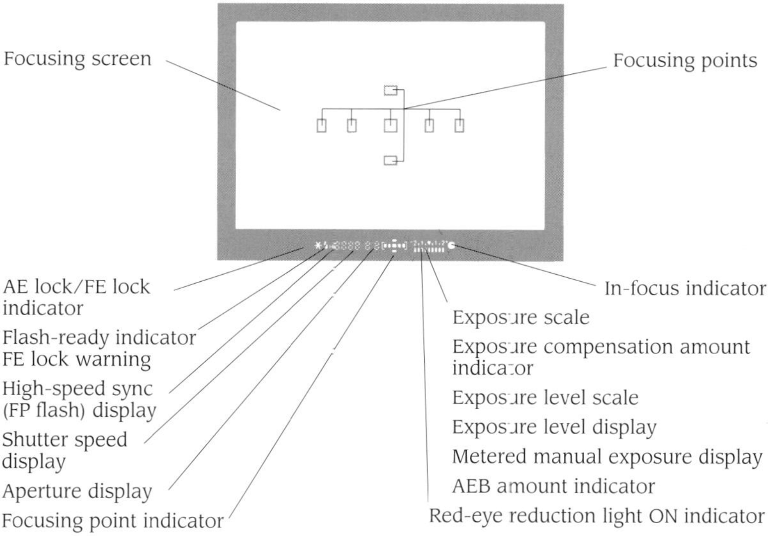

Diagram 4

The beep

You will soon notice that your EOS 300 – Rebel 2000 beeps at you from time to time. This is to confirm correct focus – the green in-focus symbol appears in the viewfinder, also. Although this is very useful, you may find that there are times when the beep is infuriating or intrusive– perhaps during wildlife photography, or at a concert. Because of this, the EOS 300 – Rebel 2000 allows you to turn off the beep in Creative Zone modes.

To do this, press the Function Button until the arrow in the LCD panel lines up with the sound symbol. A '1' will appear in the display. Now turn the Input Dial to change the '1' to a '0'. Wait six seconds, press the shutter button partway or turn the Command Dial to lock the setting. The beep is now disabled. To turn the beep back on, repeat the procedure and set '1'.

The beep sounds during self-timer operation (see Chapter 15). This is also silenced by turning off the beep.

Chapter 3

Getting your EOS ready for action

Before you can go and take photographs with your EOS 300 – Rebel 2000, there are a few essential preparations that you must make to get it ready for action.

Power to your EOS

Your EOS 300 – Rebel 2000 contains state-of-the-art electronics. In effect, it is a camera, computer, flashgun and lightmeter all rolled into one. So, not surprisingly, the camera needs electricity for it to work.

The EOS 300 – Rebel 2000 is normally powered by a brace of small, but powerful, CR2 lithium cells. These batteries are not cheap, as you will find out when you go to buy some, but when you consider what they have to power, the compact cells become good value for money. Practically every feature of the EOS 300 – Rebel 2000 requires power from the batteries, for instance; the motordrives to wind and rewind the film, the built-in flashgun and its metering system, the shutter, exposure meter, lens motors to control aperture and focusing, the LCD and viewfinder display, and the camera's microprocessor.

Installing the batteries

The batteries slip into a compartment in the base of the camera. To get into this, release the catch with your finger nail and open the hinged cover. Make sure that the batteries are fitted the right way round – you'll see Positive and Negative symbols inside the battery compartment lid. (see diagram 5). Finally, ensure that the cover is firmly closed.

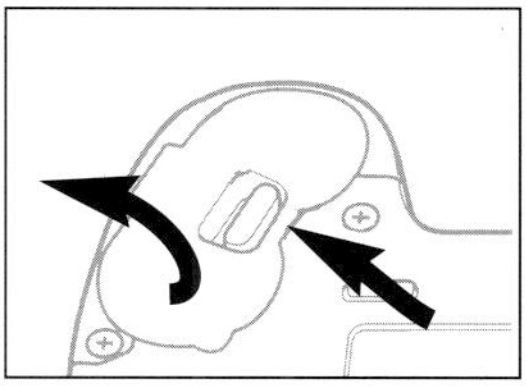

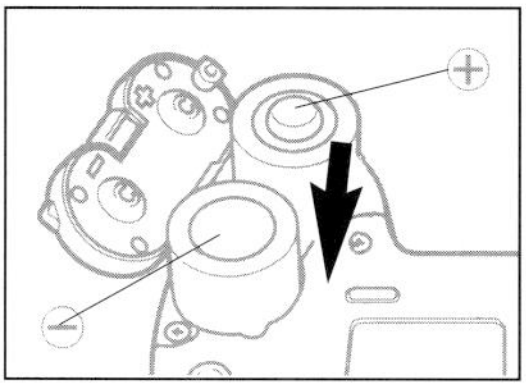

Diagram 5:
Unclip the battery compartment cover with your finger nail and insert the batteries as shown.

Checking the batteries

Your EOS 300 – Rebel 2000 will not work if the batteries are dead, so it is important to keep an eye on their state. The LCD panel displays a battery check indicator; get into the habit of looking at this every time that you use the camera. The indicator is a battery symbol. When it is totally black, the batteries are at full power. When only half the symbol is black, the batteries are partly used, but still have plenty of life in them. When the symbol is clear, the batteries are almost exhausted – be ready to replace them. Eventually, the clear battery symbol will start to flash. This means that – although there is enough power for a correct exposure – film advance and rewind may not occur, neither may there be enough power for the lens to focus.

Do not replace the batteries as soon as the indicator becomes clear. As long as the batteries have enough life in them to power the camera, you can continue to take photographs. Don't be worried that low batteries will give incorrect exposures, either – when the camera senses that battery power is too low, it locks the shutter – you will no longer be able to take a photograph. Then, and not before, is the time to load fresh batteries.

It is a good idea to always carry a couple of spare batteries. It is annoying to be stuck with a camera you cannot use, and CR2 batteries are not available at every corner shop. But do not keep the same spare for years – batteries deteriorate with age, so always rotate your supplies.

If you are out in very cold conditions, battery performance will drop. If this happens, remove the batteries and warm them against your body before putting them back in the camera.

Maximising battery life

When you first get your EOS 300 – Rebel 2000 you will be constantly playing with it, and your friends and family will be keen to have a go too. Even if you are not one to fiddle, you need to spend time getting to know the camera controls. All this uses power, so don't be surprised when your first batteries do not last very long; accept it as an essential part of the learning procedure.

Once the novelty has worn off and you know your EOS 300 – Rebel 2000 like the back of your hand, its batteries will last a lot longer. If you want to maximise battery life, do not use the built-in flash unnecessarily, avoid activating the viewfinder display and focusing the lens if you do not intend to take a photograph, and use the depth-of-field preview sparingly.

Some people remove the batteries from their camera when they are not using it, thinking that will help to conserve them. But, in fact, continuously removing and replacing batteries can actually decrease battery life. Just remember to switch the camera to Lock before you put it away, otherwise the shutter button may get depressed in your camera case. This will switch on the viewfinder display and drain the batteries very quickly.

If you use your camera a lot, or you travel to areas where 2CR5 batteries are hard to find, it is possible to power the camera with readily available AA batteries using the optional Battery Pack BP200 – see Chapter 18.

Attaching the lens

Your EOS 300 – Rebel 2000 is an interchangeable lens camera. This means that the lens can be removed from it, allowing you to choose one that most suits the type of photograph you are taking – see Chapter 17 for more information on lenses.

You probably bought your camera with a standard zoom lens – with a focal length of 28-80mm or 35-105mm. This is ideal for general photography and, if you do not have another lens, you will have no reason to remove it.

The camera and lens come separately. The lens mount on the front of the camera is protected by a body cap. This is removed by turning it anticlockwise. The rear of the lens is also covered with a cap that is removed in a similar way. To mount the lens, line up the red dots on the rear of the lens and front of the camera, and bring the two components together. Turn the lens clockwise until it clicks firmly into place.

To remove the lens, press the lens release button on the front of the camera and turn the lens anticlockwise (Diagram 6).

When the camera does not have a lens on it, always replace

the body cap to stop dirt from entering. Avoid changing lenses in damp or dirty conditions. Never touch the mirror inside the camera. If the mirror gets dirty, use a blower brush to remove loose particles. If this is not enough, use a Prophot lens cloth to gently clean the mirror.

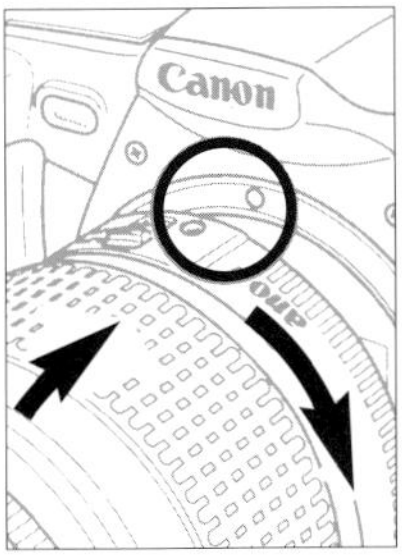

Diagram 6:
Press the lens release button and turn the lens anticlockwise to remove it.

The neck strap

Your EOS 300 – Rebel 2000 comes with a neck strap. This humble little accessory is often overlooked, but it can protect your camera from damage or loss. The strap is the most convenient way to carry your camera, and catches it if you should accidentally drop it.

Most people, when confronted by a strap and EOS camera, are puzzled as to how to put the two items together. It is not obvious how the strap attaches, but study Diagram 7 and it will become clear. Make sure that you pull the ends of the strap after attaching it, to check that it is firmly in place. This is the only safe way to attach the strap, so don't try inventing your own way of doing it – you may put your camera at risk!

If you wish, you can replace the standard strap with an Op/tech camera strap that features a unique weight reduction system to make your camera feel much lighter and more comfortable to carry. Ask your photo dealer for details.

Now that you have attached the neck strap, always use it. If you drop your EOS, the strap will only be of use if it is around your neck!

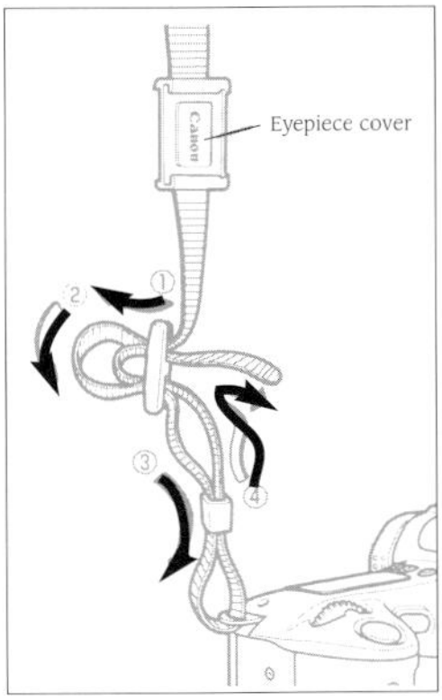

Diagram 7:
This is the one and only way to attach the neck strap to your camera.

Loading a film

Your EOS 300 – Rebel 2000 is of no use if it does not have a film in it. But don't load one immediately; take time to read this book and the instruction book to get to know the camera controls – leaving the film out gives you a chance to try out the camera without wasting frames.

When you feel ready to take some photographs, make sure that the Command Dial is not set to Lock, then open the camera by pressing the camera back release button (Diagram 8a) (get into the habit of looking through the little window in the back to make sure that there is not a film loaded before opening it). Now drop the film cassette bottom first into the space on the left of the camera (Diagram 8b), and pull the film leader across to the orange mark (Diagram 9). Close the camera back. You will hear the sound of a motor as the camera winds the film out of the cassette.

This may seem strange if you have used other SLR cameras – the EOS 300 – Rebel 2000 uses what is known as a prewind system. This winds all the film out of the cassette when you first load a film and then, each time you take a photograph, the film is wound back into the cassette frame by frame. The great advantage of the prewind system is that, if you accidentally open the camera back when a film is loaded, the valuable exposed films are safely inside the light-tight cassette and so will not be fogged.

As the film is being wound out of the cassette, the film counter in the LCD panel will count up. If you've loaded a 24-frame film it will go up to '24', while the display will read '36' with a 36-exposure film.

A film cassette symbol also appears in the LCD panel when a film is loaded. If this is flashing, the film has failed to load; open the camera back and check that the leader lines up with the orange mark before trying again.

After you have shot the last frame, the camera automatically rewinds the film leader into the cassette, ready to be removed for processing. When the film is fully rewound, the symbol in the LCD panel flashes, telling you that it is safe to open the camera back.

For more information on film rewind, turn to Chapter 10.

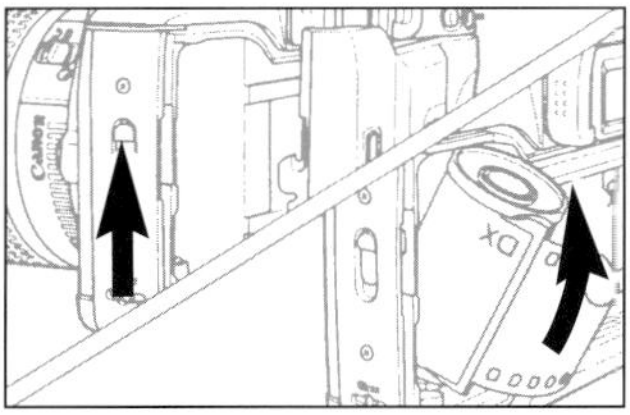

Diagram 8a:
Open the camera back by releasing the catch on the end of the body.

Diagram 8b:
Insert the film bottom end first.

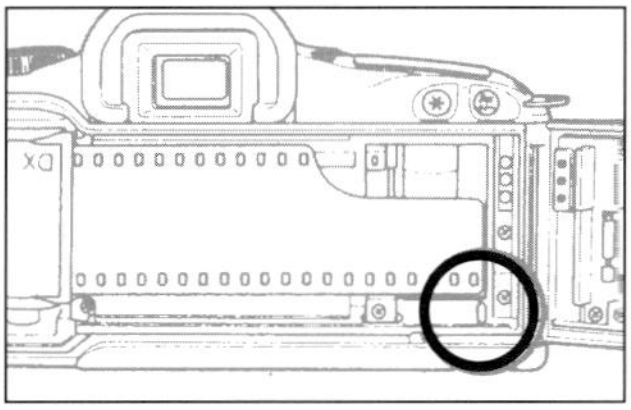

Diagram 9:
Pull the film leader across to the orange mark and then close the camera back.

Film speed

The black and silver checks on a 35mm film cassette is a DX Code. This tells the camera what ISO setting to make, so there is normally no need to set the film speed yourself. The code also contains information on film length and type.

After the film has loaded, the ISO setting appears briefly in the LCD panel. Get into the habit of checking this each time that you load a film. Very occasionally, the camera fails to read the DX Code and therefore sets the wrong film speed.

If this happens, you must set the film speed yourself. You also have to do this if you are using a non-DX Coded film, or wish to alter the manufacturer's speed.

To manually set the film speed, turn the Command Dial to the 'ISO' position . The same letters, together with the current film speed, will appear in the LCD panel. Now turn the Input Dial until the desired film speed (between ISO 6 and 6400) shows in the panel. Turn the Command Dial to another position to save the setting. This value will be overridden when another film is loaded.

Infrared film

Your camera instruction book states that infrared film cannot be used in the EOS 300 – Rebel 2000. This is because the camera's ultra-quiet film winding mechanism uses an infrared system to count the sprockets as the film travels through the counter. This can fog infrared film. However, the fogging is limited to the bottom 15% of the frame, and it may be much less with some films. Therefore, so long as you allow for this, you can use infrared film in your EOS 300 – Rebel 2000.

Chapter 4

Full Auto and PIC modes – taking your first pictures

Now that you have loaded your EOS 300 – Rebel 2000 with a film and batteries, and attached the lens, you are ready to take photographs. If you have never used an EOS before, you may be bewildered by the camera controls, but you have no need to worry. Look at the Command Dial and you will see a green square (Diagram 10). Turning the dial to this position sets Full Auto mode. This turns your EOS into a foolproof point-and-shoot camera – all you have to do is aim it in the right direction and press the shutter button; the camera does everything else for you.

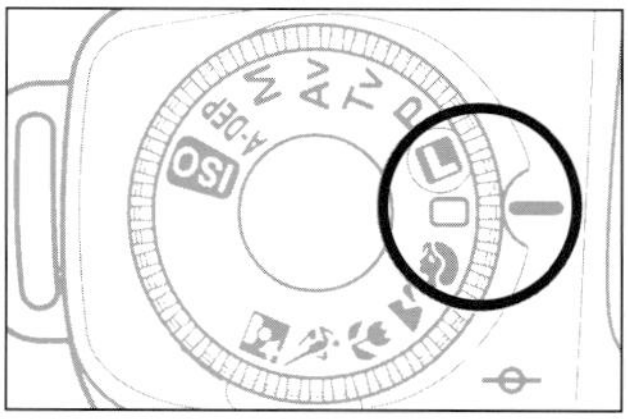

Diagram 10:
Turn the Command Dial to the green square to set Full Auto mode.

Full Auto

Bring the camera to your eye and move around until the subject appears in the viewfinder. If necessary, adjust the lens' zoom setting. Now half press the shutter button. The image snaps sharply into focus and you will hear a beep that tells you that the camera has successfully focused; a green circle appears in the viewfinder to confirm focus. Gently, but firmly, fully press the shutter button to take the photograph. Congratulations – you have shot your first EOS picture. Easy wasn't it?

Full Auto mode looks after focusing, exposure metering, aperture and shutter speed. In low light, or outdoors in contrasty lighting, the built-in flash pops up when the camera senses it is required. Because Full Auto is designed to be foolproof, it is not possible to use functions such as Exposure Compensation and Auto Exposure Bracketing. Focusing is set to AI Focus, film advance to Single Frame and metering to Evaluative – it is not possible to alter any of these. Neither can you control when the flash fires.

Full Auto is so good that you may wonder why the camera needs other shooting modes! However, as you learn more about photography, you will start to want to take more control over the picture-taking process, and you will find that Full Auto does not always give the result that you want.

But as you progress, don't forget about Full Auto mode – it is ideal for parties, family snapshots and other occasions when you don't want to worry about setting the camera. It is also useful when family and friends want to use your EOS.

PIC modes

Full Auto is good, but the settings that the camera makes in this mode have to be a compromise to ensure acceptable results with all subjects. That is why the EOS 300 – Rebel 2000 also offers Program Image Control – commonly known as PIC modes.

PIC modes are similar to Full Auto in that the camera makes all the decisions for you, but the difference is that each PIC mode customises these settings to suit a particular subject.

Five PIC modes are available – Portrait, Landscape, Close-up, Sports and Night Scene. These are set by turning the Command Dial to the relevant icon.

If you are an experienced photographer, you may be surprised by some of the settings that the camera chooses in PIC modes. This is because the modes are designed to be foolproof and extreme settings are avoided. These are explained under the heading for each PIC mode.

Portrait

Most of us take pictures of people – family, friends, or just interesting characters that we meet. Portrait mode, indicated by an icon of a woman's head (Diagram 11), helps to ensure that these pictures are flattering to the subject.

A wider lens aperture than normal is set to limit the depth-of-field and throw the background out-of-focus. This ensures that your subject stands out against their surroundings. For best results, use a lens setting of at least 80mm – 100mm or 135mm is even better. Long focal lengths help to limit depth-of-field and put a comfortable distance between you and your subject.

Because people move about, Portrait mode sets film advance to Continuous. So if you keep your finger on the shutter button, the camera takes a series of pictures in quick succession – make sure that you have plenty of film! The built-in flash pops up and fires if it is required. Alternatively, you can use a Speedlite; this will fire for every shot.

Don't expect the camera to set the widest aperture, it is more likely to chose a mid-range setting to ensure that there is enough depth-of-field to allow for poor focusing. As you become more experienced you will want to change to Aperture Priority mode (see Chapter 5) for your portrait photography.

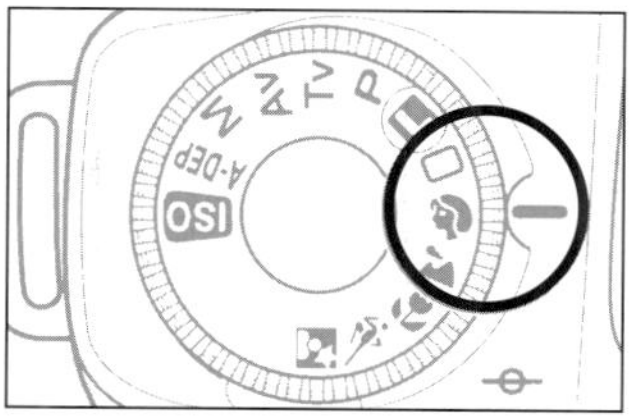

Diagram 11:
Turn the Command Dial to the icon of a woman's head to set Full Auto mode.

Landscape

Landscapes are all around you – even if you live in a city you can find stunning vistas if you look. Landscape PIC mode is depicted by an icon of a mountain with a cloud (Diagram 12). Turn the Command Dial to this setting to photograph distant scenes.

Most landscape pictures benefit from a small aperture to give maximum depth-of-field. However, this may lead to a long shutter speed being set, so Landscape PIC mode generally sets a smallish aperture that still allows a fast enough shutter speed for hand-held photography. If you require the smallest aperture, set the camera to Aperture Priority mode (see Chapter 5) and be prepared to use a tripod or monopod.

Wide-angle lenses settings, such as 28mm or 35mm, are ideal for many landscapes because they increase depth-of-field and take in a large part of the scene. But don't forget that successful landscape shots can also be taken with telephoto lenses – don't be afraid to break the rules.

Because landscapes do not generally move, this PIC mode sets One Shot focusing and Single Shot frame advance with Evaluative metering. The built-in flash will not fire – no flashgun is powerful enough to illuminate a large scene! For this reason you should not have a Speedlite mounted for landscape pictures – it will fire if it is switched on and may cause the picture to be incorrectly exposed.

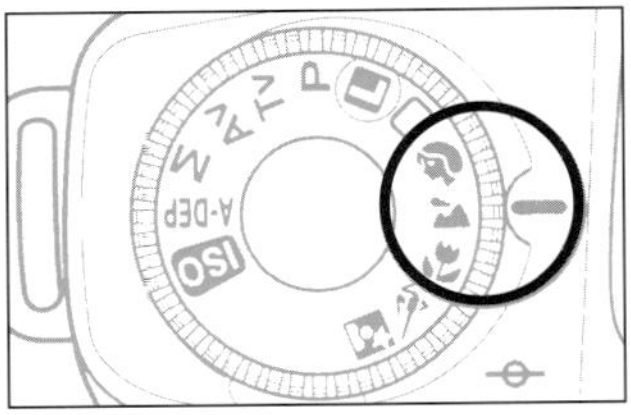

Diagram 12:
Turn the Command Dial to the icon of a mountain and a cloud to set Landscape mode.

Sport

Sport PIC mode sets your EOS to shoot a variety of fast moving subjects, not just sports. Turn the Command Dial to the icon of a runner (Diagram 13) and your EOS sets a faster shutter speed than normal to help freeze the movement of an action shot. AI Servo focusing and Continuous film advance are also selected, together with Evaluative metering.

The built-in flash does not fire in Sport mode. As with Landscape mode, using a Speedlite may not give the results that you expect.

You will probably want to use a long focal length lens setting to enable you to get close to the action, and a high shutter speed also helps to avoid camera shake spoiling your pictures – long lenses not only magnify the image, they also magnify camera shake.

Sport mode may not set the fastest possible shutter speed. Being a beginner's setting, it ensures that the aperture is small enough to give reasonable depth-of-field and therefore make sure that the subject is sharp. Use Shutter Priority mode (see Chapter 5) if you want to set the fastest possible shutter speed to freeze action.

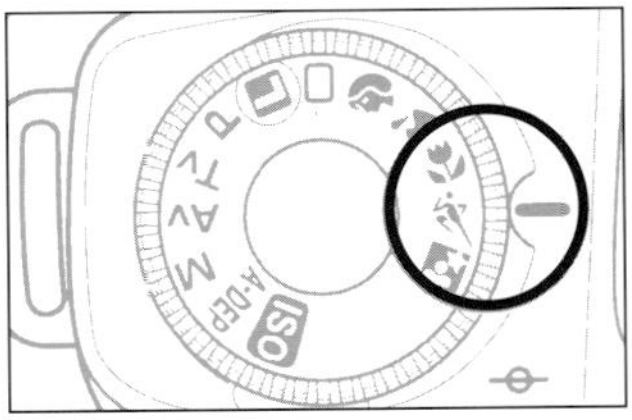

Diagram 13:
Turn the Command Dial to the icon of a runner to set Sport mode.

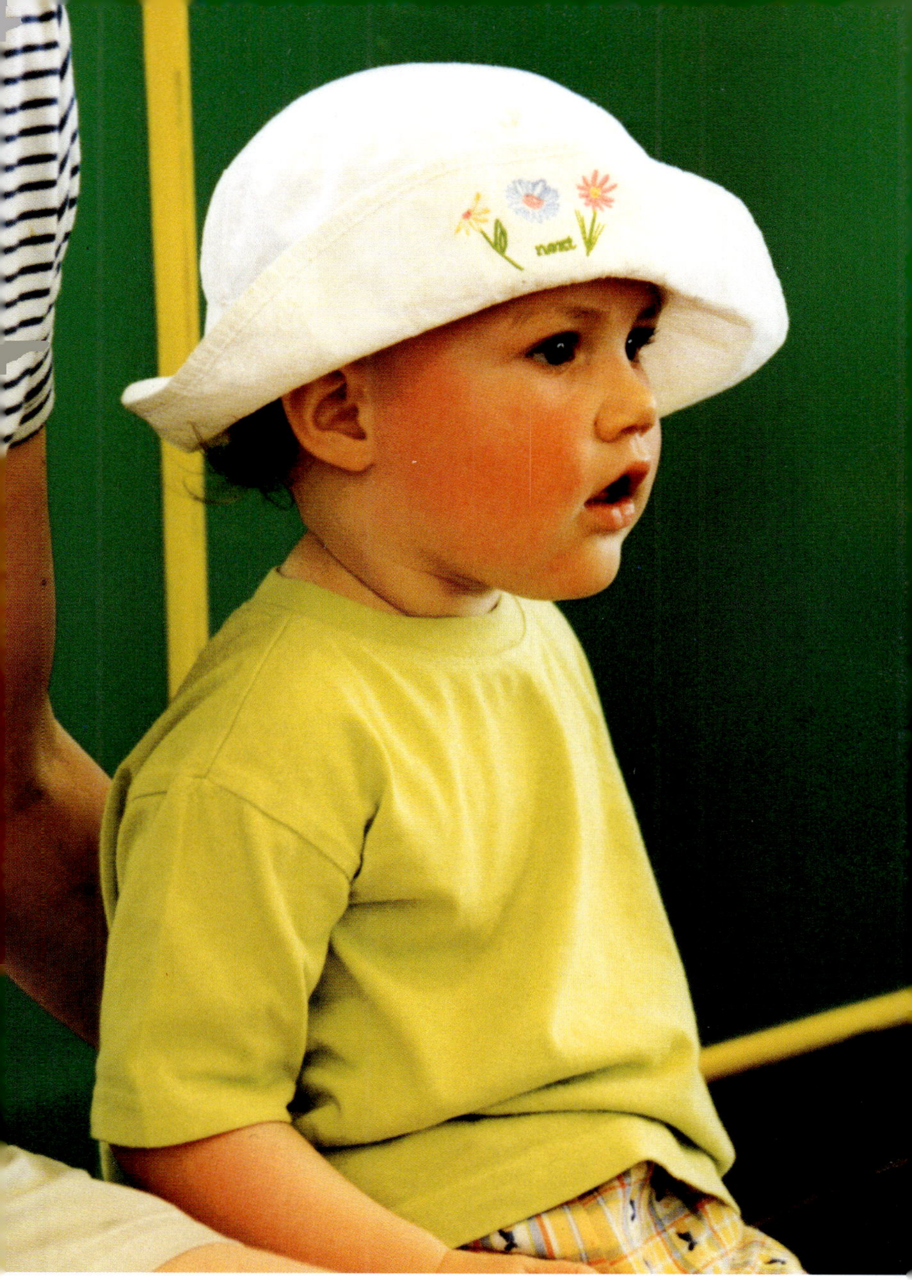

Often, the best child portraits are those where the subject is not aware that they are being photographed. This candid shot of a little girl was taken with a long telephoto lens.

Photograph: Philip Raby

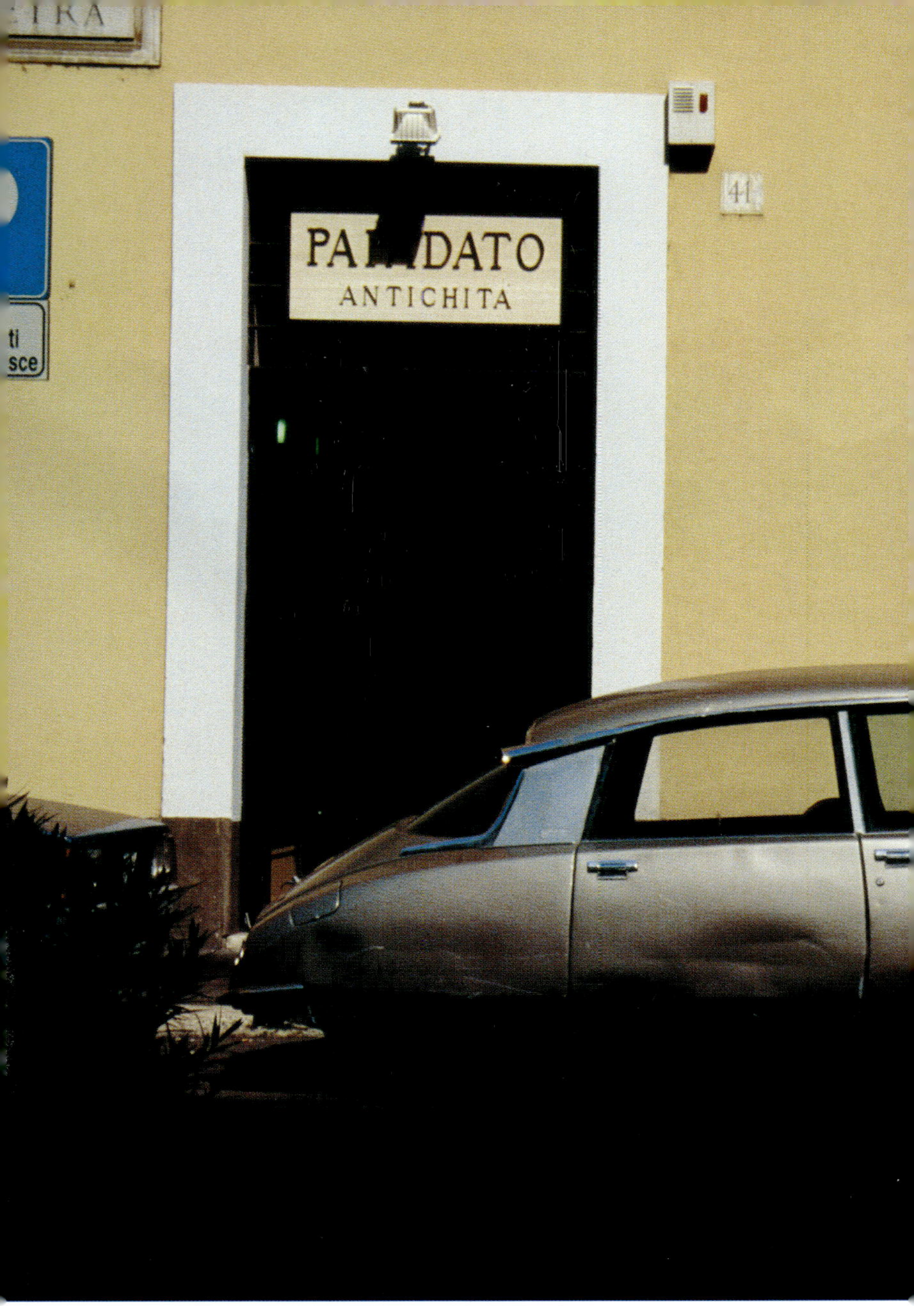
ANTICHITA
41

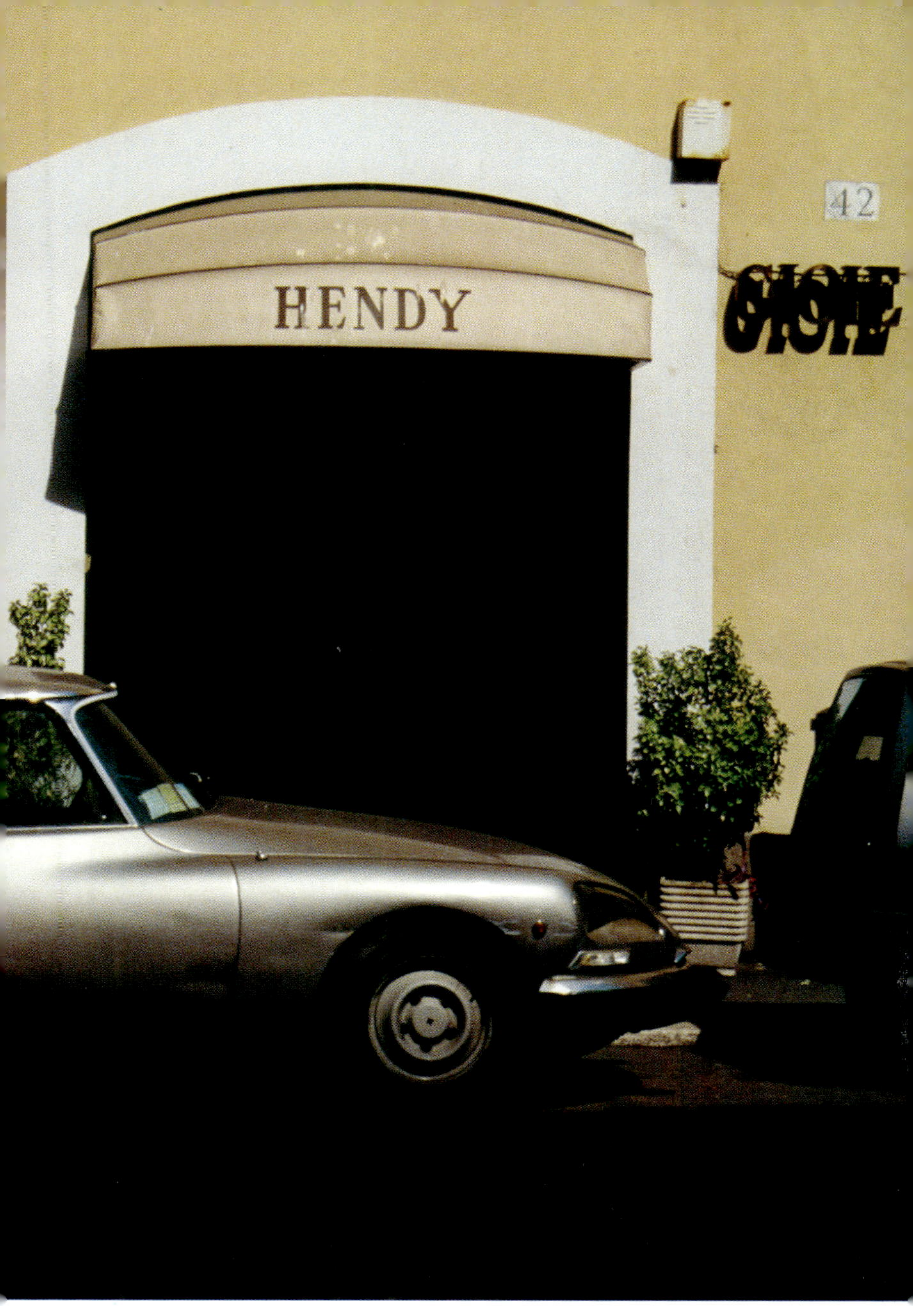

This old Citroen was spotted on a Rome side street. The bright sun has created harsh shadows that gives the picture a truly continental feel.

Photograph: Philip Raby

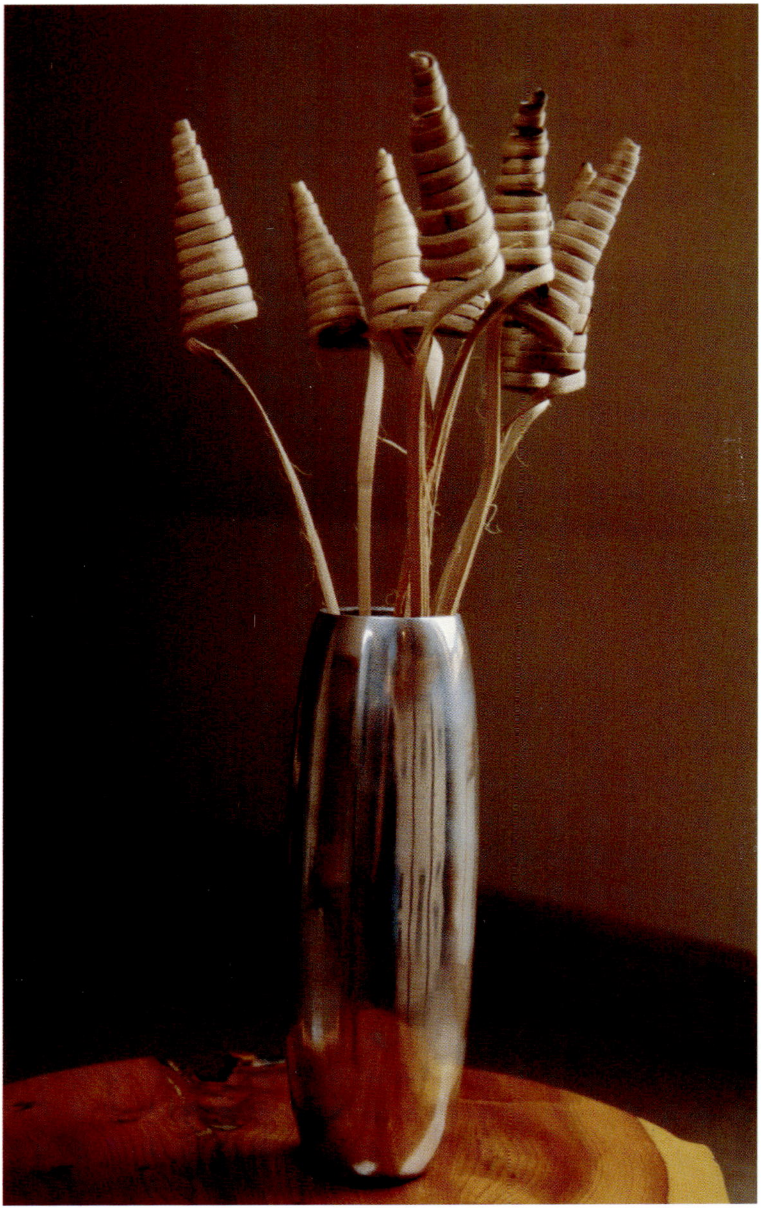

Don't automatically use flash for all your indoor photographs. This impromptu still-life was taken using available light coming through a nearby window. Flash would have lost this subtle illumination.

Photograph: Philip Raby

Close-up

Close-up photography opens up a whole new world. Everyday objects in your own backyard become exotic subjects to point your EOS at. Many EF lenses focus close enough for low-power close-up work – look for a yellow flower on the lens barrel.

For straightforward close-up photography with one of these lenses, turn the Command Dial to the icon of a flower (Diagram 14). This mode chooses a smallish aperture to increase depth-of-field, which decreases as you get closer to a subject. But very small apertures are not set in close-up mode because they may lead to shutter speeds too long for hand-held photography.

Focusing is set to One Shot, and film advance to Single Frame in Close-up mode.

The built-in flash fires if it is required. If you are using a Speedlite, this will always fire.

To get in closer to your subject, you will need a special EF Macro lens (see Chapter 17), extension tube or a supplementary close-up lens (see Chapter 18).

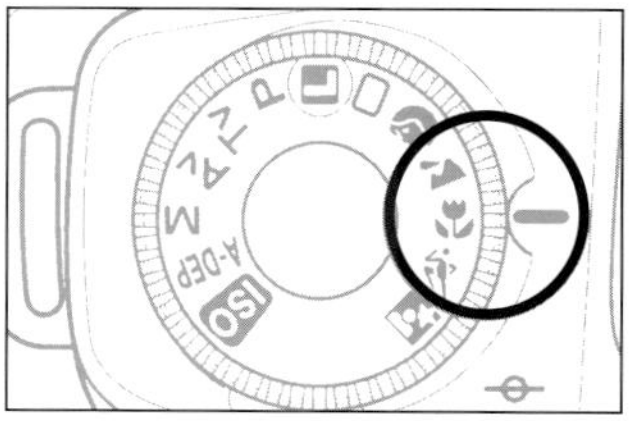

Diagram 14:
Turn the Command Dial to the icon of a flower to set Close-up mode.

Night Scene

Night Scene mode is designed for taking flash portraits at night that retain some background detail. Night Scene is set by turning the Command Dial to the icon of a figure with a star behind (Diagram 15).

Examples of pictures taken with Night Scene mode may be a person standing on a bridge with city light behind, or a child at the funfair with illuminated rides behind.

To understand Night Scene mode you need to know that flash exposure is determined by two things – aperture and flash output. The ambient (natural) light is determined by aperture and shutter speed. Shutter speed has no affect on the flash exposure. Also, bear in mind that the light from the flash falls off with distance, so although a close subject will be lit by the flash, more distant ones will not be.

In most camera shooting modes, the camera will try to balance the flash and ambient exposures, but only while there is enough light for hand-held shutter speeds. If the ambient light drops below EV 10, the camera will ignore the ambient light and concentrate on the flash exposure. The background may then go black, although the subject will still be correctly exposed by the flash.

In Night Scene mode, the camera will set a shutter speed that will expose for the background. This means that you need to mount the camera on a tripod, monopod or other firm support to avoid camera shake spoiling the picture. If you have the optional Remote Switch RS-60E3 (see Chapter 18), use it to fire the camera.

Night Scene mode can be used with either the built-in flash or a Speedlite. Remember, though, that it can only show background detail if there is some light to be recorded. If the background is pitch black, there is nothing the camera can do to make it visible!

An alternative to Night Scene mode is to set Aperture Priority mode (see Chapter 5).

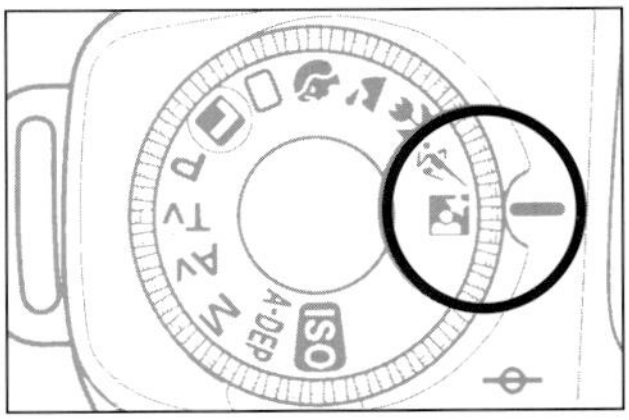

Diagram 15: Turn the Command Dial to the icon of a figure with a star behind to set Night Scene mode.

Chapter 5

Beyond the basics–Creative Zone modes

Now that you have mastered Full Auto and PIC modes you will want to take more control over your photography. Look at the Command Dial; on the opposite side of the Lock position to the PIC modes are the Creative Zone settings. These give you the control that you want, while still letting you make use of the camera's sophisticated metering systems.

The main difference between Full Auto and PIC modes and the Creative Zone settings is that the latter give you access to Exposure Compensation (Chapter 8), Auto Exposure Bracketing (Chapter 8), AE Lock (Chapter 7) and Multiple Exposures (Chapter 11).

Let's look at each Creative Zone mode in detail.

Program

In Program mode – the 'P' setting on the Command Dial (Diagram 16) – your EOS 300 – Rebel 2000 selects both an aperture and a shutter speed to give a correct exposure for the conditions.

You may think that this sounds the same as Full Auto mode, and in some ways it is. The exposure settings that the camera makes are identical, but the difference is that you can alter these settings by using other camera functions, such as Exposure Compensation.

Unlike Full Auto mode, the built-in flash does not automatically fire in Program mode. If you wish to use the flash, you must activate it manually; it then behaves the same way as when Full Auto is set.

Program mode is ideal for a range of photographic situations where you do not wish to set a specific aperture or shutter speed. In fact, it is a good mode to leave your camera in for taking most of your pictures. When you use Program mode, keep

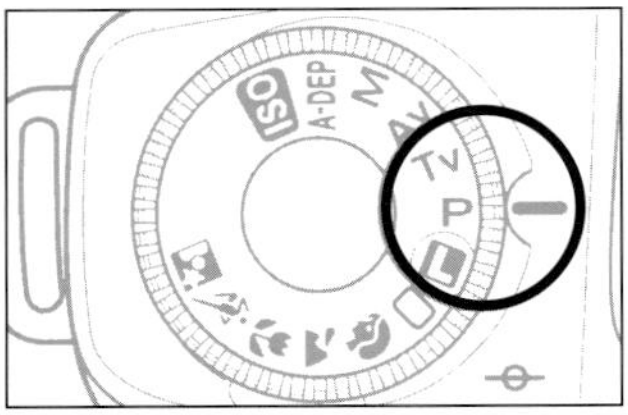

an eye on the viewfinder display so that you can check that the aperture and shutter speed are suitable for the effect that you desire.

Diagram 16: Turn the Command Dial to 'P' to set Program mode.

Program Shift

The most powerful way that you can alter the exposure settings made by the camera in Program mode is to use Program shift.

This under-used feature allows you to alter the aperture and shutter speed set by the camera, while still retaining a correct exposure. It relies on the fact that increasing the shutter speed by one stop halves the amount of light reaching the film, and opening the aperture by the same amount doubles the amount of light. So as the shutter speed increases, the aperture opens to compensate. In other words, you shift the settings.

Program Shift provides a useful way for beginners to start controlling shutter speed and aperture without switching to Aperture Priority or Shutter Priority modes. It can also be used by more experienced photographers in rapidly changing lighting conditions when there is not enough time to switch to another mode.

Program Shift is very simple to use. After you half press the shutter button to focus and take an exposure reading, the camera displays the chosen aperture and shutter speed in the viewfinder. If you then turn the Input Dial, say, two clicks clockwise (when looking from the back of the camera), the shutter speed increases by one stop. At the same time, the aperture opens by one stop to ensure that the exposure remains constant. For instance, if the camera sets 1/125 second at f8, turning the Input Dial two clicks clockwise shifts the settings to 1/250 at f5.6. This gives exactly the same exposure. Turning the Input Dial the other way decreases the shutter speed and sets a smaller aperture.

It is not possible to set a shutter speed or aperture that will not give a correct exposure – if you turn the Input Dial beyond the widest aperture, Program Shift stops operating. This means you cannot set an incorrect exposure.

Remember that if you choose a long shutter speed, you may need to use a tripod or monopod to avoid camera shake spoiling your photograph.

Do not use Program Shift if you wish to take a number of photographs at the same aperture and shutter speed – the settings are lost after you have pressed the shutter button. Program Shift does not operate during flash photography, with either the built-in flash or a Speedlite.

Shutter Priority

Turn the Command Dial to 'Tv' (Diagram 17) to set Shutter Priority mode (Tv stands for Time Value – a little used photographic expression). In this mode you choose the shutter speed by turning the Input Dial until the desired setting appears in the viewfinder and LCD panel. The camera then sets an aperture that will ensure a correct exposure.

However, the camera may not be able to give a correct exposure. For instance, in dim conditions, you are unlikely to be able to set a shutter speed of, say, 1/2000 sec – even the widest aperture setting will not allow enough light to reach the film. Or in very bright conditions, the camera may not be able to set a small enough aperture if you have chosen a longer shutter speed, say 1/4 second. If the light is too bright or too dark for a correct exposure, the viewfinder display will flash. You must turn the Input Dial to alter the shutter speed until the flashing stops. If you do not do this, you will still be able to fire the shutter, but the photograph will not be correctly exposed. Light conditions change, so keep an eye on the display to make sure that it is not flashing. If the light drops, you may have to set a longer shutter speed.

Use Shutter Priority mode when shutter speed is important. For instance, during action photography when a fast speed will help to freeze action. Or when you are using a telephoto lens and a shutter speed of at least 1/focal length is needed to minimise camera shake during hand-held photography. For instance, if you are using a 200mm lens, the shutter speed should be 1/200 second or faster.

This mode is also useful when you wish to set a long shutter speed to blur movement – for instance, when photographing running water.

Remember to keep an eye on the aperture setting – too wide an aperture limits depth-of-field, whereas a small aperture makes everything in the frame appear sharp. It is up to you to decide which effect you require.

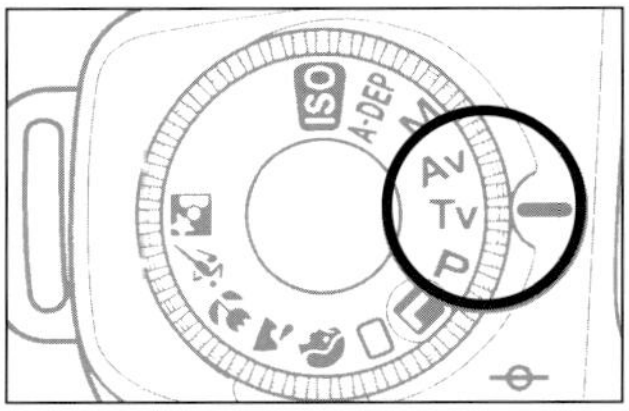

Diagram 17:
Turn the Command Dial to 'Tv' to set Shutter Priority mode.

Aperture Priority

Aperture Priority mode is the opposite of Shutter Priority – you select the aperture and the camera sets a corresponding shutter speed. Switch your EOS 300 – Rebel 2000 to Aperture Priority mode by turning the Command Dial to 'Av' (Aperture Value) (Diagram 18).

The aperture is set by turning the Input Dial until the desired value appears in the viewfinder and LCD panel. If the viewfinder and LCD panel flash, the camera is unable to set a shutter speed that will give a correct exposure. When this happens you must alter the aperture by turning the Input Dial until the flashing stops. If you do not do this, the shutter will still fire, but the photograph will be incorrectly exposed.

In Aperture Priority mode, it is important to keep an eye on the shutter speed. If you set a small aperture, such as f5.6, the camera may set a long shutter speed to ensure that enough light reaches the film. If this happens, you must mount the camera on a tripod, monopod or other firm surface to avoid camera shake spoiling the photograph. Alternatively, set a wider aperture to bring the shutter speed up to hand-holding levels.

Use Aperture Priority mode when you want to limit depth-of-field. For instance, setting a wide aperture, such as f4, limits the depth-of-field and throws backgrounds, or foregrounds, out-of-focus. This is a useful technique for portrait photography because it gives you a sharp face against a blurred background. A short telephoto lens, such as 100mm, further limits depth-of-field and so is ideal for portrait work.

Aperture Priority mode is also useful when you require maximum depth-of-field to ensure that as much of the subject as possible appears sharp in the picture – landscape photography, for example. Also, it is the ideal mode for close-up and macro photography. As you get closer to a subject, depth-of-field becomes more limited, so you need to set a small aperture to give as much sharpness as possible.

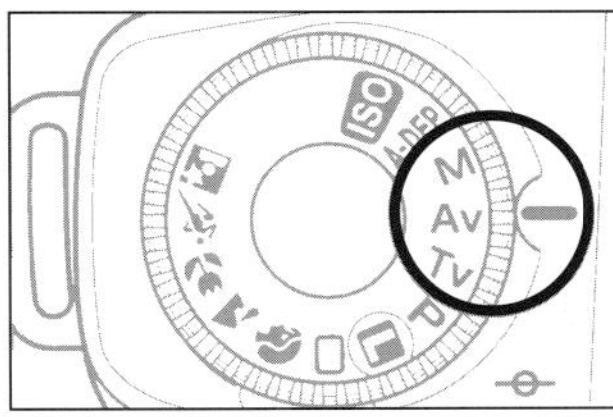

Diagram 18:
Turn the Command Dial to 'Av' to set Aperture Priority mode.

Manual

You may be surprised that your EOS 300 – Rebel 2000 has a Manual mode. After all, it gives such good results when you leave it to get on with the job, why bother setting the aperture and shutter speed yourself? To be honest, there are only a few occasions when you need to set Manual, but it is a mode worth knowing about.

When you turn the Command Dial to 'M' (Diagram 19), your EOS 300 – Rebel 2000 relinquishes control of shutter speed and aperture, leaving you to make both settings. But don't worry, the camera exposure meter remains active to guide you if you wish.

The shutter speed is adjusted by turning the Input Dial. The aperture is set by pressing the 'Av' button on the back of the camera and then rotating the Input Dial.

When you look into the viewfinder in Manual mode and half press the shutter button to focus, the display shows a linear scale with an arrow. When this arrow is in the centre of the scale, the exposure, according to the camera, is correct. You must adjust the aperture and shutter speed to achieve this. If the arrow blinks at -2 or +2 stops, the picture will be under or overexposed by more than two stops.

Exposure Compensation is not possible in Manual mode.

The best way to use Manual mode is to first decide what is more important – shutter speed or aperture. For instance if you decide that you require maximum depth-of-field, set a small aperture such as f22. Now half press the shutter button and look at the viewfinder display. If necessary, adjust the shutter speed until the arrow under the linear scale is centralised.

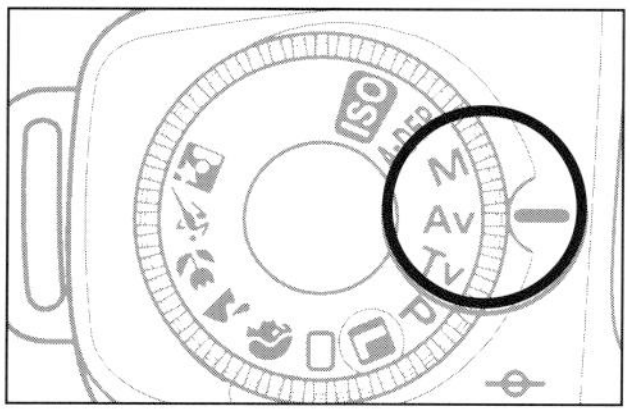

Diagram 19:
Turn the Command Dial to 'M' to set Manual mode.

Here are some situations when Manual mode is useful:

Learning about photography

Your EOS 300 – Rebel 2000 gives incredibly accurate exposures in Full Auto, PIC and Creative Zone modes; the latter allowing you to override the settings. But taking total control of exposure from time to time is an excellent way to learn more about photography. It also slows down the picture-taking process, forcing you to spend more time thinking about each shot, rather than clicking madly away. Then when you return to using another mode, you will have a better idea of what the camera is doing and why it makes the settings it does. Don't forget that you can make use of the camera's built-in exposure meter in Manual mode.

Using a separate light meter

The metering systems of your EOS 300 – Rebel 2000 is so accurate that there is really no need to use a hand-held light meter. However, you may prefer to use one for some of your pictures, in which case you must put your camera into Manual.

Taking a reading from a grey card

Your EOS 300 – Rebel 2000 metering system assumes that the subject you are photographing is a mid-tone – an average of dark and light tones – and will set an exposure that will make the photograph appear the same brightness. A typical mid-tone is a white person's skin or a grass lawn.

A grey card is a board with a mid-tone grey surface. This can be positioned so that it receives the same light as the subject, and an exposure reading taken from it, making sure that it fills the frame in the viewfinder. By putting the camera into Manual, you can hold this reading when you remove the grey card and recompose the subject.

Grey cards are most commonly used when photographing paintings and other flat artwork.

Using a single exposure setting

There are situations when the light is constantly changing, but you want to leave the shutter speed and aperture unaltered. In an automatic setting, the camera will alter the settings to suit the changing light.

For instance, at a pop concert there are often flashing coloured lights in the background, while the performers are lit by a more constant white light. By putting your EOS 300 – Rebel 2000 in Manual, and taking a partial meter reading from a performer's face, you can ensure that all the frames will be exposed the same and not affected by the background lighting.

Using non-dedicated flashguns

When using non-dedicated flashguns and studio flash units, your EOS 300 – Rebel 2000 must be set to Manual. See Chapter 14 to find out more.

Macro flash photography

When taking macro or close-up photographs with a Speedlite flashgun, you should set the camera to Manual; flash control will still be automatic.

Bulb setting

Normally, the longest shutter speed possible with your EOS 300 – Rebel 2000 is 30 seconds. However, when your EOS 300 – Rebel 2000 is in Manual mode , you have access to a unique setting – Bulb.

To set Bulb, first make sure that the camera is in Manual mode and then turn the Input Dial towards the longest shutter speeds, when you get to 30 seconds, keep going – the LCD panel will display 'buLb'.

When your EOS 300 – Rebel 2000 is set to Bulb, the shutter remains open as long as the shutter button is kept fully depressed. That means that there is no limit to the length of your exposures.

Bulb is used in very low light, when even 30 seconds is not long enough for a correct exposure, although it can also be used for setting shorter exposures. The camera must be mounted on a sturdy tripod to ensure that it doe not move during the exposure. Ideally, you should use a remote release (see Chapter 18) to activate the shutter – it is hard to keep your finger pressed down on the shutter button without moving the camera. You need to use a stop-watch or count 'elephants' to time Bulb exposures.

In case you are wondering, the term bulb comes from the days when photographers used pneumatic releases to fire their cameras. These consisted of long tubes with rubber bulbs on the end.

Chapter 6

Depth-of-field

Depth-of-field is something that you must learn to control in order to take better photographs. Before looking at how your EOS 300 – Rebel 2000 lets you do this, let's find out a little about depth-of-field.

What is depth-of-field?

Depth-of-field is the distance between the nearest and farthest points in a photograph that appear acceptably sharp. It is not, as many people think, the amount of the picture that is in focus. A lens only focuses on one point at a time – anything closer or farther from the lens is out-of-focus but may appear to be sharp.

Depth-of-field depends partly on aperture. When you set a wide lens aperture, such as f4, depth-of-field is minimal, and only the area that the lens is focused on appears sharp. However, by stopping down to a small aperture, such as f22, much more of the scene appears sharp, even though it is still technically out-of-focus.

Focal length has an effect on depth-of-field. As the focal length of a lens increases, depth-of-field decreases. Therefore, a wide-angle lens is able to give more depth-of-field than a long focal length lens.

Another factor influencing depth-of-field is lens-to-subject distance. As the lens gets closer to the subject, depth-of-field decreases. This becomes particularly apparent during macro photography when the lens may be just a few centimetres from the subject. Therefore, you must set the smallest possible aperture to ensure that the subject appears acceptably sharp.

Focusing and depth-of-field

Some people think that setting a small aperture means that they do not have to worry too much about focusing. But depth-of-field does not increase the area that is in focus, only the amount of acceptable sharpness. You should always take care to focus on the most important part of your subject.

If you are photographing a scene that you wish to be sharp from foreground to background, use a wide-angle lens, select Aperture Priority mode, set a small aperture and focus one-third of the way into the picture. This will ensure maximum depth-of-field. Remember that a small aperture may lead to a long shutter speed, so be ready to use a tripod or monopod.

Depth-of-field mode

Although Aperture Priority mode is suitable for controlling depth-of-field, the EOS 300 – Rebel 2000 boasts a Automatic Depth mode. To select this, turn the Command Dial to the 'A-DEP' setting (Diagram 20).

Now look at the subject and decide the nearest and farthest points you wish to appear sharp in the photograph. Look through the viewfinder and move the camera until these parts of the subject are covered by the camera's focusing points. When you half-press the shutter button, these points will light up red. The camera then selects an aperture that will give sufficient depth-of-field, as well as focusing at the optimum distance. A shutter speed is set that will ensure a correct exposure with the selected aperture.

If the aperture value flashes in the viewfinder, the amount of depth-of-field required is not possible – the camera will give as much as it can. You may be able to get around the problem by moving away from the subject – depth-of-field increases with distance. Alternatively, use a wider focal length lens setting – wide-angle lenses give more depth-of-field than telephoto ones.

If the shutter speed flashes at 30 seconds and the maximum aperture flashes, there is not enough light to take the photograph in Depth mode. Increase the lighting or load a faster speed film. Conversely, if the shutter speed flashes at 1/2000 second together with the minimum aperture, there is too much light. Load a slower speed film or attach a neutral density filter to the lens (a neutral density filter reduces the amount of light that reaches the film without affecting it in any other way).

In Automatic Depth mode, your EOS 300 – Rebel 2000 may set a long shutter speed to compensate for a small aperture. Keep an eye on the viewfinder display and if the shutter speed becomes too long for hand-held photography mount the camera on a tripod or monopod.

Do not try and use flash in Automatic Depth mode; it will not work and the camera will revert to Program mode. Also, this mode cannot be used when the lens is set to Manual focus.

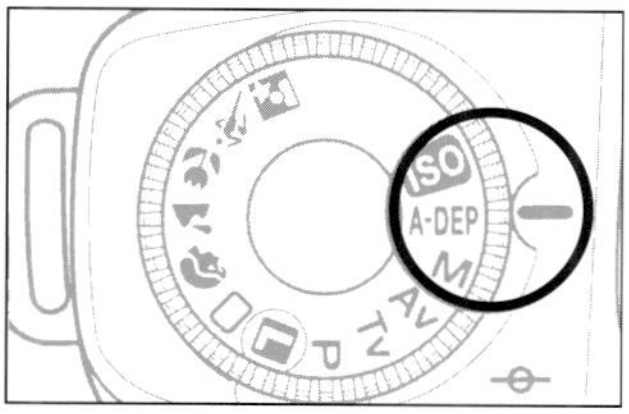

Diagram 20:
Turn the Command Dial to 'A-DEP' to set Depth-of-field mode.

Depth-of-field Preview

When you look through the viewfinder of your EOS 300 – Rebel 2000, you will not see the effect of the aperture on depth-of-field. This is because the aperture diaphragm is always wide open until the moment that you press the shutter button, when it closes down the pre-selected amount. If it did not do this, the viewfinder image would be too dark to see clearly at small apertures.

However, your EOS 300 – Rebel 2000 allows you to stop down the aperture, prior to taking the photograph, to enable you to see how much of the subject will appear sharp in the photograph.

To do this, press the Depth-of-field Preview button on the side of the lens mount (Diagram 21).

Note that, if the widest aperture has been set, pressing the Depth-of-field Preview button will have no effect on the viewfinder image.

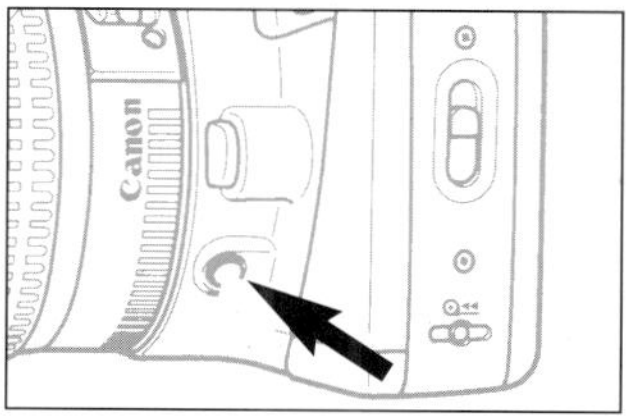

Diagram 21:
Press the Depth-of-field Preview button to stop down the lens to see the effect of aperture on depth-of-field.

Depth-of-field the lazy way

If all this sounds like too much bother, many photographers get excellent results by using a simple rule-of-thumb. Set a small aperture for maximum depth-of-field, and a wide aperture to limit depth-of-field. Not very scientific, but it works!

Chapter 7

Metering modes

For a good photograph, the film in your camera must receive just the right amount of light. Too little and the photograph will be dark (underexposed), too much and it will be too bright (overexposed). The amount of light that reaches the camera depends on two things – the shutter that controls the amount of time that the film is exposed to light, and the aperture that determines the brightness of the light which reaches the film.

Back in the old days, before electronic cameras, photographers had to either guess the aperture and shutter speed, using their experience and guides supplied with films (sunny weather; 125th at f11, cloudy weather; 60th at f4), or, for more accurate results, use a hand-held exposure meter.

But your EOS 300 – Rebel 2000 uses state-of-the-art electronics to measure the amount of light passing through the lens and reaching the film. This is called Through-The-Lens, or TTL, metering and means that poorly exposed photographs are almost a thing of the past. Even the most inexperienced photographer can achieve superb results at the push of a button.

The EOS 300 – Rebel 2000 offers three types of exposure metering – Evaluative, Centre-weighted Average, and Partial.

Evaluative

This is the mode set by the camera in all shooting modes except Manual.

Evaluative metering divides the subject area into zones, and a meter reading is taken from each zone (Diagram 22). The camera's microprocessor analyses these readings and compares them with sample readings stored in memory. It is able to assess whether the subject is backlit or particularly bright or dark, and sets the shutter speed and aperture accordingly. What's more, it assumes that the area that you have focused on is to be correctly exposed, and biases the exposure to the active focus point.

Evaluative metering copes with most lighting conditions, and you will find very few occasions when you cannot trust it to get on with the job.

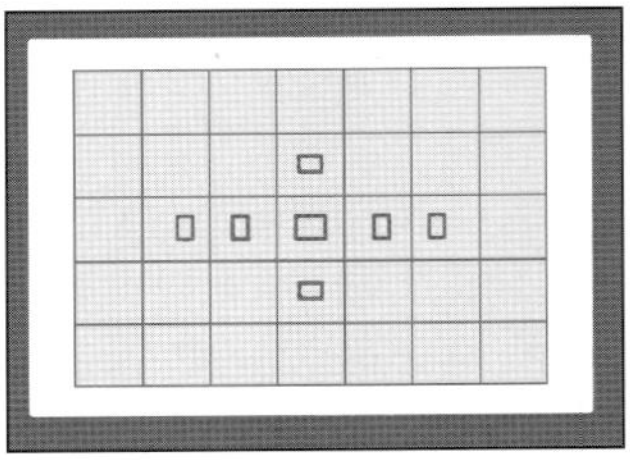

Diagram 22:
Evaluative metering divides the subject area into zones.

Centre-weighted Average

Before the days of Evaluative metering, Centre-weighted Average was the metering system used in most Canon cameras. It takes a reading from the whole of the scene (diagram 23), but with a bias to the central area, the assumption being that the main part of the subject will be in the centre of the picture.

Centre-weighted Average gives good results with most subjects, but may be confused with backlit, bright, or dark subjects, as well as off-centre ones.

The EOS 300 – Rebel 2000 only uses Centre-weighted Average when it is set to Manual mode. It is not possible to select it in any other mode.

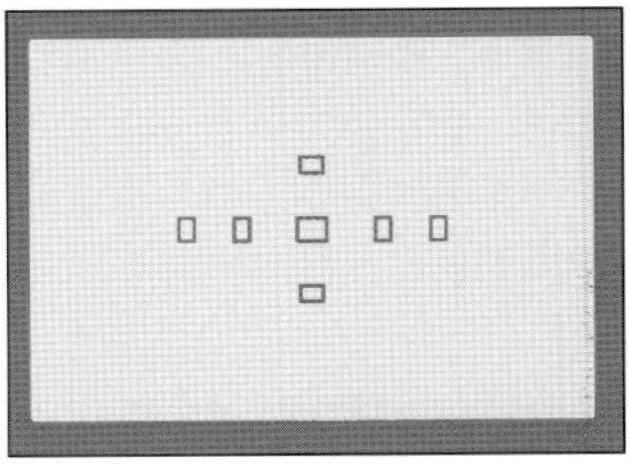

Diagram 23:
Centre-weight Average metering take a reading from the whole scene.

Partial metering

As its name suggests, Partial metering takes an exposure reading from just a small part of the subject area. Normally, the reading is taken from the centre 9.5% of the viewfinder image – around the centre focus point (Diagram 24).

Partial metering is used when the subject that you are photographing is surrounded by an expanse of bright or dark areas. Although Evaluative metering can cope with most situations, it may be confused by a dominant or dark background and expose for that rather than the subject. Partial metering allows you to take a reading just from the part of the subject that you wish to reproduce as a mid-tone. It is very useful for portraits.

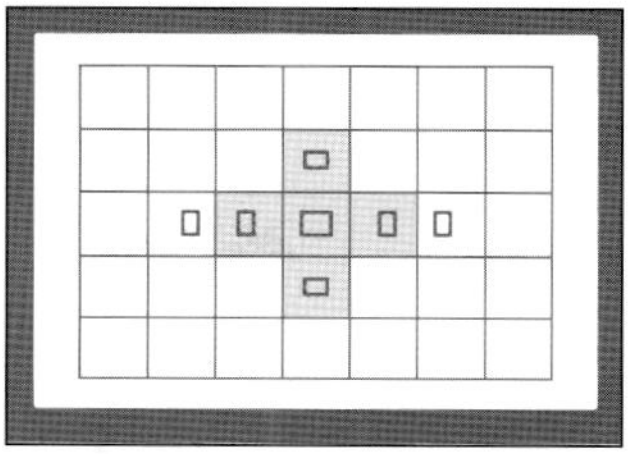

Diagram 24:
Partial metering takes a reading from just the centre of the frame.

How to use Partial metering

Partial metering can only be used when AE Lock is activated. AE Lock (also known as Exposure Lock) allows you to take a light reading from one part of a scene, and hold it while you recompose the photograph.

To use AE Lock, point the camera at the area that you wish to be exposed as a mid-tone. Now press the AE Lock button on the back of the camera (Diagram 25). The exposure settings will lock, even if you take your finger off the button. To cancel the setting, press the button again to take another reading, switch off the camera, or wait six seconds for the viewfinder display to cancel.

Use Partial metering and AE Lock in situations when the subject is surrounded by a light or dark background. For instance, when photographing a white person against a dark wall, Evaluative metering will try to expose for the wall and give an overexposed face. Therefore, take a Partial reading from the face, and hold it with AE Lock while you recompose the picture. A white person's skin is a mid-tone, so the camera will ensure that is correctly exposed.

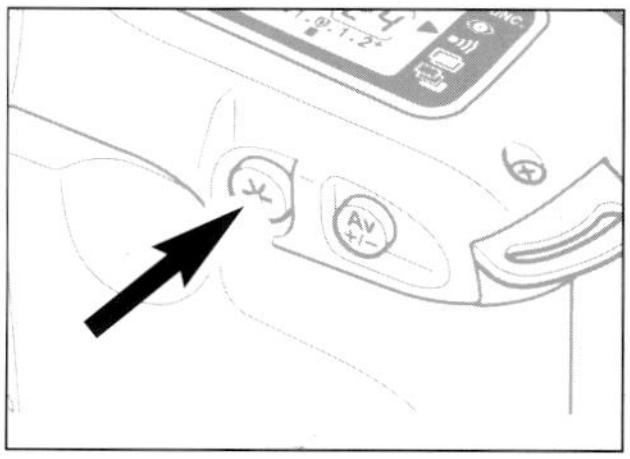

Diagram 25:
Press the AE Lock/Partial metering button to activate Partial metering and hold the reading.

Stop-down metering

Stop-down metering is not mentioned in the camera instruction book and most photographers are unlikely to need it. It is only required when you have a non-dedicated lens or accessory attached to your EOS 300 – Rebel 2000. This may be a mirror lens, slide copier, Canon Auto Bellows, or a Canon FD mount lens attached with an adaptor.

A dedicated lens is able to communicate with your camera through a series of gold-plated contacts and tell it what its maximum aperture is. A non-dedicated accessory is unable to do this, so the camera has to meter the light in a different way to ensure a correct exposure. This system is called stop-down metering.

Your EOS 300 – Rebel 2000 automatically switches to stop-down metering mode when a non-dedicated lens or accessory is attached in Aperture Priority mode. The camera displays an aperture of f0.0 and will set a suitable shutter speed. If you are using a Speedlite flashgun, set the camera to Manual and choose a shutter speed no faster than 1/90 second: the flash will adjust to give a correct exposure.

Chapter 8

Exposure Compensation

You can be certain that your EOS will give superb results in most situations. However, just occasionally, you need to override the camera's selected shutter speed and aperture. You can do this by setting Manual mode (see Chapter 5), but it can be easier to use Exposure Compensation in Creative Zones. This allows you to alter the settings made by the camera by up to ±2 stops in 1/2 stop intervals.

The camera does this by altering the shutter speed, aperture, or both. In Shutter Priority mode, the aperture changes, in Aperture Priority mode, the shutter speed alters, and in Program mode, either or both settings change.

Exposure Compensation is not possible when the camera is set to Manual.

How to set Exposure Compensation

Before setting Exposure Compensation, make sure the camera's set to a Creative Zone mode. Next, focus and take an exposure reading in the normal way by half pressing the shutter button.

Within four seconds of doing this, press and hold down the Exposure Compensation button (+/-) on the back of the camera (Diagram 26). At the same time, turn the Input Dial until the desired amount of compensation appears on the bar graphs in the LCD panel and viewfinder display (Diagram 27). Moving the arrow below the scale to the left decreases the exposure in 1/2 stop increments down to -2 stops. Moving the arrow to the right increases the exposure up to +2 stops in the same increments.

Remember that Exposure Compensation remains set until you cancel it by setting the bar graphs in the LCD panel and viewfinder are centralised. Always check that Exposure Compensation is not set when it is not required.

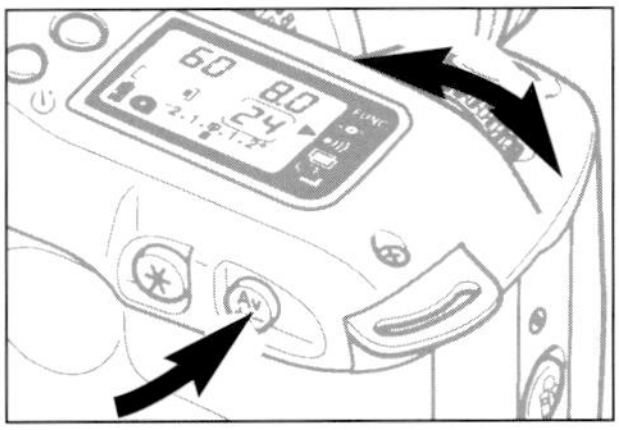

Diagram 26:

Press the Exposure Compensation button and turn the Input Dial to set the required amount of Exposure Compensation.

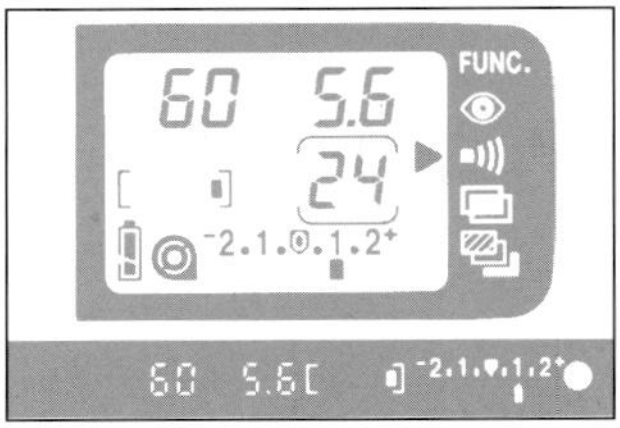

Diagram 27:

The amount of Exposure Compensation set is displayed in the bar graph in the viewfinder and on the LCD panel.

When to use Exposure Compensation

As you develop as a photographer you will learn to recognise times when you need to alter the exposure set by the camera. Here are some common situations:

White subjects

You know that snow, for instance, is white. However, the light meter in your EOS 300 – Rebel 2000 does not; it assumes that any subject is a mid-tone. Therefore, it reproduces snow, or any other white or light subject, as a murky grey. So, if your subject is predominantly white, set exposure compensation to +1.5 stops to ensure a pure white result.

Black subjects

The opposite of white objects is a pile of coal, or any other dark or black subject. The camera again assumes that the subject is a mid-tone and exposes accordingly, giving a grey result. To ensure black tones in the photograph, underexpose the film by about -1.5 stops.

Increasing colour saturation

The ISO film speed rating suggested by the film manufacturer is the one to use in most situations. However, colour slide film occasionally benefits from slight underexposure. This increases the saturation of bright, deep colours. Until you have learnt when to use this technique, take two shots – one with Exposure Compensation and a second picture without. Colour print (negative) film does not benefit from underexposure in this way.

Soft focus

A range of lenses and accessories is available to degrade the sharp image formed by your camera. The reason for doing this is to create a soft focus image for portraits and dreamy effects.

Many soft images are enhanced by slight overexposure to wash out the highlights and give a light, dreamy atmosphere.

Auto Exposure Compensation (AEB)

If you don't know whether to under or overexpose a shot, or indeed whether compensation is required, don't worry. You can set your EOS 300 – Rebel 2000 to take three frames – one with minus compensation, one without compensation, and a third overexposed by a chosen amount. When you get the film back from the processors, you can then chose which frame is the best. If you think that shooting three frames is wasteful, it is much better than taking one unsuccessful picture – especially if the shot is unrepeatable.

This feature is called Auto Exposure Compensation (AEB) and is used mainly with colour slide film – negative film has a wider exposure latitude and slight changes to exposure are less noticeable.

How to set AEB

To set AEB, press the Function button on the top of the camera until the arrow on the LCD panel points to the AEB symbol (Diagram 28). Now turn the Input Dial until the desired bracketing amount appears in the LCD panel (Diagram 29). The amount of compensation can be set in 1/2 stop intervals to two stops. For instance, if AEB is set to 1.0, three pictures will be taken; one at the correct exposure determined by the camera, one under exposed by one stop and a third overexposed by one stop.

To take the pictures, press the shutter button all the way in the usual way.

AEB is not automatically cancelled after taking a photograph, so you can take a series of pictures using the facility. After you have finished using AEB, cancel it by pressing the Function button until 'AEB' appears in the LCD panel and then turn the Input Dial to return the bracketing amount to zero.

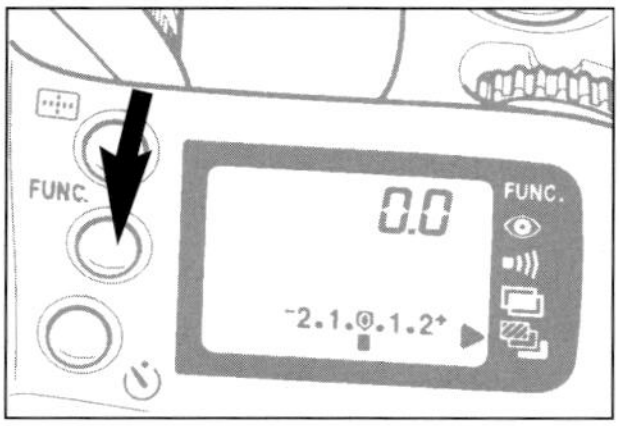

Diagram 28:

Press the Function button until the arrow in the LCD panel points to the AEB symbol to activate Auto Exposure Bracketing.

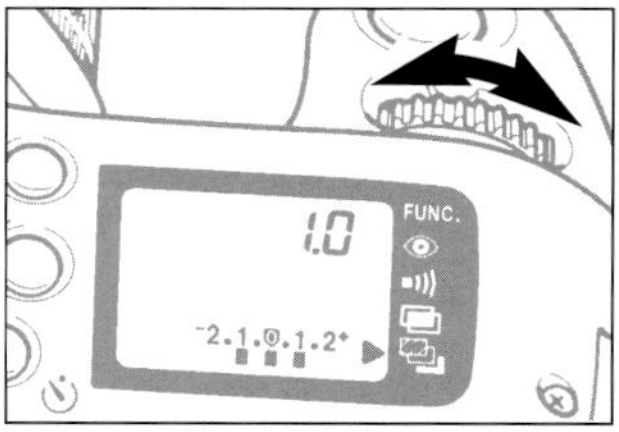

Diagram 29:

Turn the Input Dial to set the required amount of Auto Exposure Bracketing.

Combining AEB with Exposure Compensation

Because AEB is a form of exposure compensation, you may be surprised to know that it can be used in conjunction with the camera's Exposure Compensation feature. You should do this when you know which direction the compensation should be set, but are unsure how much to set.

For example, white subjects should be overexposed, so it would be a waste of a frame to set AEB to give an underexposed shot. The answer is to set the required AEB setting and then set Exposure Compensation to twice that amount. For instance, set AEB to +0.5 stops and Exposure Compensation to +1 stop. The camera will then give three images, overexposed by +0.5, +1 and +1.5 stops.

Chapter 9

Multipoint focusing

Your EOS 300 – Rebel 2000 features a seven-point focusing system. Less advanced cameras simply focus on the centre of the viewfinder image, but this is no good if the subject is to one side of the frame; which is where you will often want to put it for a balanced composition.

The seven-point system allows you to focus on a subject in the centre of the frame, to one side or the other, or above or below the centre. The focus point can either be chosen automatically by the camera or manually by you.

Automatic point selection

Automatic point selection is always used in Full Auto, PIC and A-Depth modes mode; it is not possible to select the focus point yourself in these modes.

Automatic point selection assumes that the area closest to the camera is the part of the scene that you wish to be in focus. If you think about it, most of your photographs have the main subject in the foreground.

Although this system is ideal for most photographs, it may not always give the result that you desire. For instance, you may be photographing a landscape framed by trees. In this situation the camera would focus on the trees rather than the main part of the scene. So it is important to always keep an eye on the area that the camera is focusing on. If the camera is not doing what you want, switch to a mode that allows manual point selection, or use Focus Lock.

Manual point selection

Manual point selection allows you to choose a focus point yourself.

This can be useful in some situations. For instance, in sports photography the main subject is likely to be always in the centre of the frame, so you can select the centre focus point. Alternatively, with practice you can quickly switch from one point to another as you are composing a shot.

To manually select a focus point, press the Focus Point Select button and turn the Input Dial until the desired point appears LCD panel. As you turn the dial the selected points scroll in the following order:

1. Auto selection (all points appear)
2. Far left point
3. Near left point
4. Upper point
5. Centre point
6. Lower point
7. Near right point
8. Far right point
9. Back to auto selection

Chapter 10

Film winding and rewinding

In the old days, photographers had to wind on the film manually between frames, either by turning a knob, or cocking a lever. Although hardly strenuous, this did slow down the picture-taking process and meant that there was a risk that the camera was not always ready for action.

The EOS 300 – Rebel 2000 uses a motor to automatically wind the film out of the cassette on loading. It is then wound back into the cassette frame by frame as you take pictures. When all the frames have been shot, the camera winds the end of the film into the cassette ready for you to remove it for processing.

Depending on the shooting mode that is set, one of two film winding modes is used: Single or Continuous

Single

Single exposure is set with Full Auto, Landscape, Close-up, Night Scene and A-Depth modes. When you fully press the shutter button, the camera takes a picture and winds on the film to the next frame ready for your next shot. But you then have to either take your finger off the shutter button or release the button to its halfway position before you can take another photograph. This is a safety device to stop you from accidentally shooting a number of frames by not releasing the button quick enough.

Single exposure mode is ideal when you just want to take one picture at a time. Use it for static subjects such as buildings and landscapes.

Continuous

In Continuous mode, the camera winds on the film and fires the shutter for as long as the shutter button is depressed. With a fresh battery in the camera, this means that you can take a photograph about every 1.5 seconds, and use a 24-exposure film in just over half a minute!

Continuous mode is used for action photography when you want to ensure that you capture the definitive moment. For instance, if you were photographing a racing car flying around a corner, you would press the shutter button just as the car reached the bend and hold it down as the vehicle negotiated the corner. The resulting sequence of pictures would show the car at various points on the curve, allowing you to choose the most suitable after the film is processed.

Your EOS 300 – Rebel 2000 sets Continuous winding in Portrait, Sports, Program, Shutter Priority, Aperture Priority and Manual modes.

Use Continuous mode with care – it can prove costly in terms of film!

Mid-roll rewind

Sometimes, you may wish to remove a film before it is finished. For instance, if you have been using a colour slide film, but wish to shoot some black-and-white shots. You could just waste the remaining frames in the slide film, but it is more frugal to wind the film back into its cassette to be used at a later date.

To do this, press the midroll rewind button on the side of the camera – it is recessed so that it cannot be pressed accidentally (Diagram 30). The film will then rewind into its cassette.

The problem with doing this is that the film leader is also wound into the cassette, making it impossible to reload. You can buy a little film retriever that hooks the end of the film from the cassette, but there is a risk that doing this will scratch the delicate emulsion. Another option is to drop the battery out of the camera just before the film is fully rewound – a technique that requires practice to get right so try it with a dud film first.

After taking a part-used film out of the camera, it is important to mark it clearly so that you don't mistake it for an unexposed film – note the number of frames that have been shot.

When you come to reuse a part-used film, you must wind it on to the first unexposed frame. To do this, set the camera and lens to Manual and choose a shutter speed of 1/2000 second and the smallest possible aperture. Put a lens cap over the lens and keep away from bright light. Now fire the shutter until the film counter in the LCD panel reaches the point that you took the film out at. Fire an extra frame just to make sure. The reason for doing it this way is to minimise the risk of light entering the camera when you fire the shutter. If you tried to fire the shutter with a lens cap on in an automatic shooting mode, the camera would try to give a correct exposure and make the shutter stay open for 30 seconds. The lens must be set to Manual otherwise the camera will try, and fail, to autofocus and the shutter will lock.

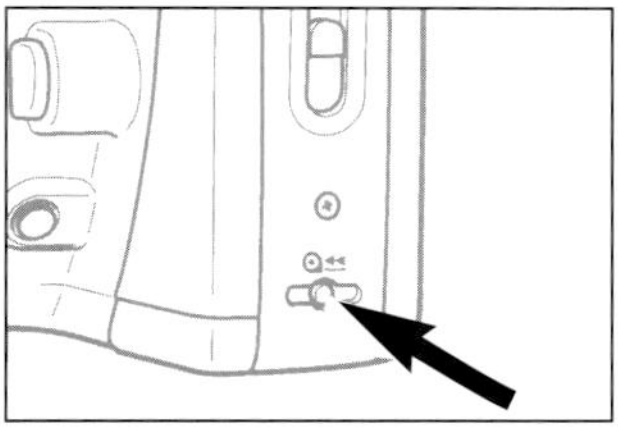

Diagram 30:

Press the Mid-roll rewind button on the side of the camera to rewind a part-used film.

Chapter 11

Multiple exposures

An interesting feature of the EOS 300 – Rebel 2000 is the Multiple Exposure facility. Normally, your camera only allows you to expose each frame once – as soon as you have taken a photograph, the film winds on to the next frame ready for the next shot. However, in Multiple Exposure mode, the film wind is cancelled, allowing you to make a number of exposures on a single frame. This gives you the ability to take a range of special effect photographs.

Setting Multiple Exposure

It is not possible to shoot multiple exposures when the camera is set to Full Auto or a PIC mode, so choose a Creative Zone setting.

Press the Function button on the top of the camera until the arrow points to the Multiple Exposure symbol in the LCD panel. A number '1' will also appear (Diagram 31). Turn the Input Dial to change this to the number of exposures you wish to make on a single frame – up to nine can be set.

When you now press the shutter button fully to take a photograph, the shutter will fire but the film will not wind on until you have made the preset number of exposures. During the sequence, the arrow will flash in the LCD panel and the number of remaining exposures is displayed. After all the exposures have been made, the camera reverts to normal operation; if you wish to take another multiple exposure photograph, you will have to make the setting again.

To cancel Multiple Exposures, press the Function button until the arrow points to the relevant symbol in the LCD panel, and turn the Input Dial to return the number of exposures to one.

Although it is very unlikely that you will want to, it is possible to make more than nine exposures on a single frame. When the set number of exposures reaches one, press the Function button and turn the Input Dial to increase the number of exposures and then start shooting again. You can do this as many times as you like to give an unlimited number of exposures!

There is no limit to how long you can wait between exposures during a sequence – you can leave the camera for hours, minutes, weeks or even months between making one exposure and the next. Just remember that Multiple Exposure mode is set and don't try to use the camera for anything else. You can also change lenses and add a Speedlite or a filter between exposures. It is possible to change shooting modes, but do not try to set Full Auto or a PIC mode – this will cancel Multiple Exposure mode.

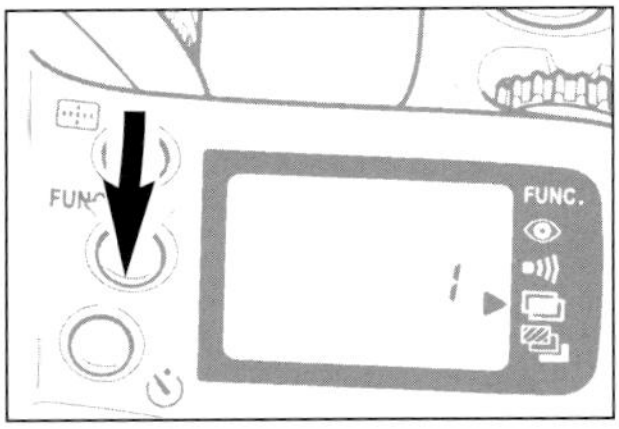

Diagram 31:

Press the Function button until the arrow in the LCD panel points to the Multiple Exposure symbol, together with a number '1'.

Using Multiple Exposure mode

If you are exposing the same scene more than once on the same frame, the film will receive too much light. To avoid this happening, decrease each exposure using Exposure Compensation (see Chapter 8). The amount of compensation required increases with the number of exposures and depends on the type of subject you are photographing. However, as a guide, set Exposure Compensation to -1 stop for two exposures, -1.5 stops for three exposures and -2 stops for four exposures.

What is Multiple Exposure mode for?

Multiple Exposure mode allows you to create all sorts of interesting and unusual effects. Here are just some ideas; you should be able think of many more.

Make a ghost image

If you want to make your friends believe that you have seen a ghost, try this simple technique.

Mount your camera on a tripod or other firm surface and set Multiple Exposure mode to two and Exposure Compensation to -1. Press the shutter button once and then get someone to step into the scene before making the second exposure.

When the film is processed you will see that the person appears transparent. This is because the first background was exposed to the film for the first exposure and then the person was exposed over the top.

If your friends aren't convinced by this, try putting a white sheet over your subject!

Add the moon to a scene

You have probably seen landscape photographs featuring a huge moon. It looks impressive, but never happens in reality – if you tried to shoot such a scene, the moon would appear far too small.

The answer is to photograph the landscape and the moon separately, using a telephoto lens for the moon shot. To be successful, the landscape must be photographed in low light so that the sky appears dark, otherwise you will get a see-through moon!

Create twins

It is possible to include the same person twice on one frame. However, if you just make two exposures with the subject in a different place, you will end up with the ghost effect described earlier. The answer is to mask half of the lens so that only half of the frame is exposed at a time. Special masks are available to fit square filter systems – your local photo dealer will be able to get you a set.

To use the mask, mount your camera on a tripod and put the mask over one side of the lens. Look through the viewfinder; you will see that half of the frame is blacked out. Ask your subject to stand on the other side so that you can see them in the viewfinder. Set Multiple Exposure mode to two and make the first exposure (you do not need to set Exposure Compensation because each half of the film is only being exposed once). Taking care not to move the camera, move the mask to the other side of the lens and ask your subject to move across so that they appear on the other side of the viewfinder, then make the second exposure.

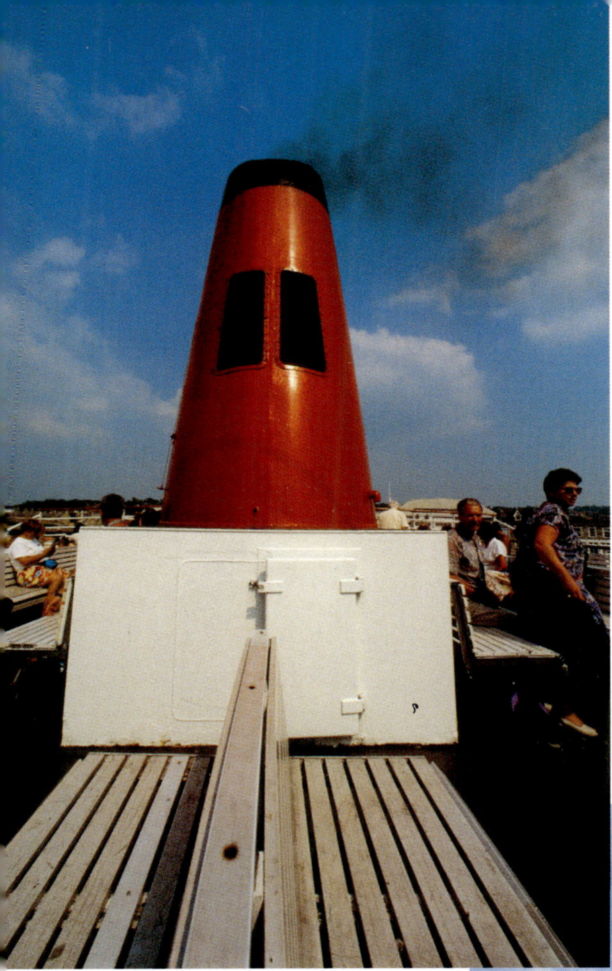

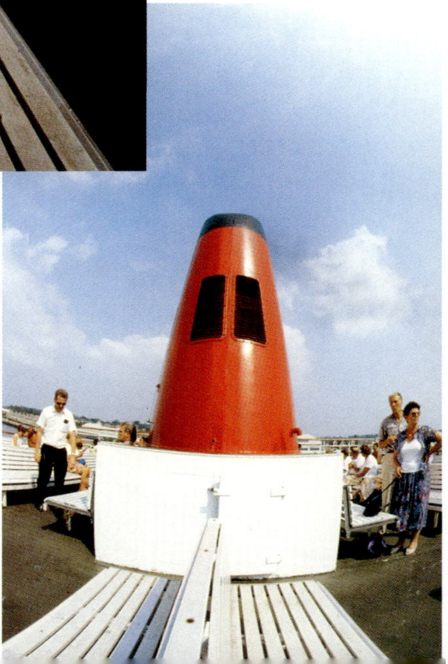

These photographs were both taken from the same point, but with different lenses. The first was shot with the EF 15mm f2.8 Fisheye; notice how the straight lines are dramatically distorted. The second, on the other hand was taken with the EF 14mm f2.8L USM; the effect is less radical, but more true to life.

Photograph: Philip Raby

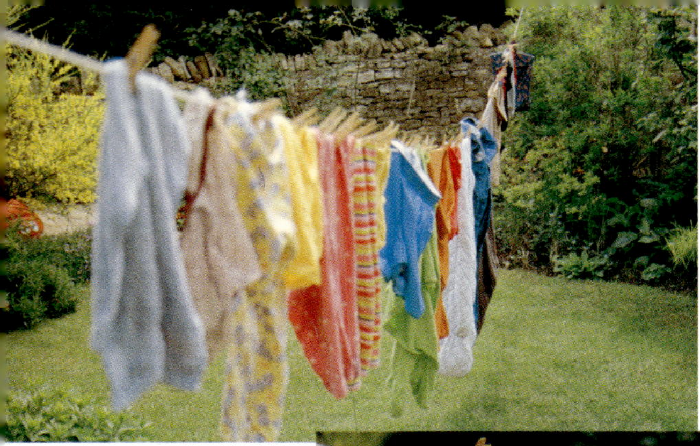

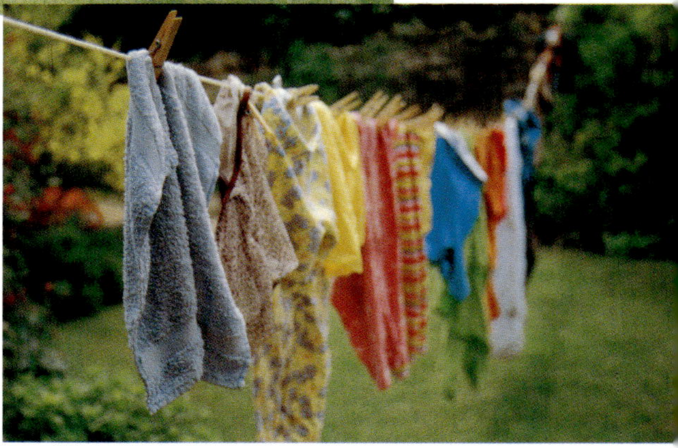

These photographs show how focusing and aperture can affect an image. The first two pictures were shot at maximum aperture. For the first, the photographer focused on the background, so most of the washing is out-of-focus. For the second, focus was shifted to the foreground so the nearest items are sharp, while the rest are blurred. The third picture was photographed with a small aperture so that everything from the foreground to the background appears sharp.

Photograph: Philip Raby

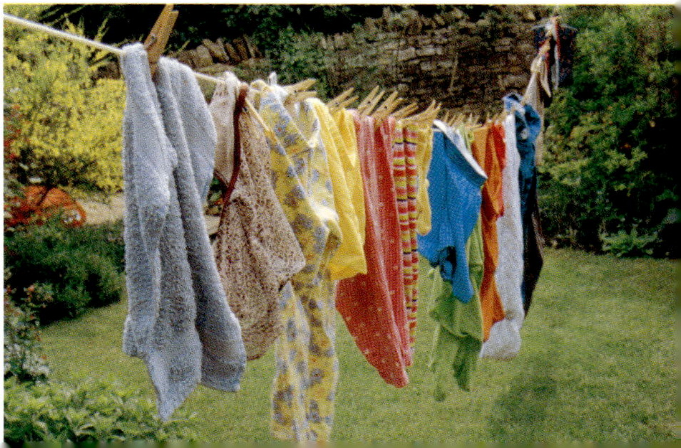

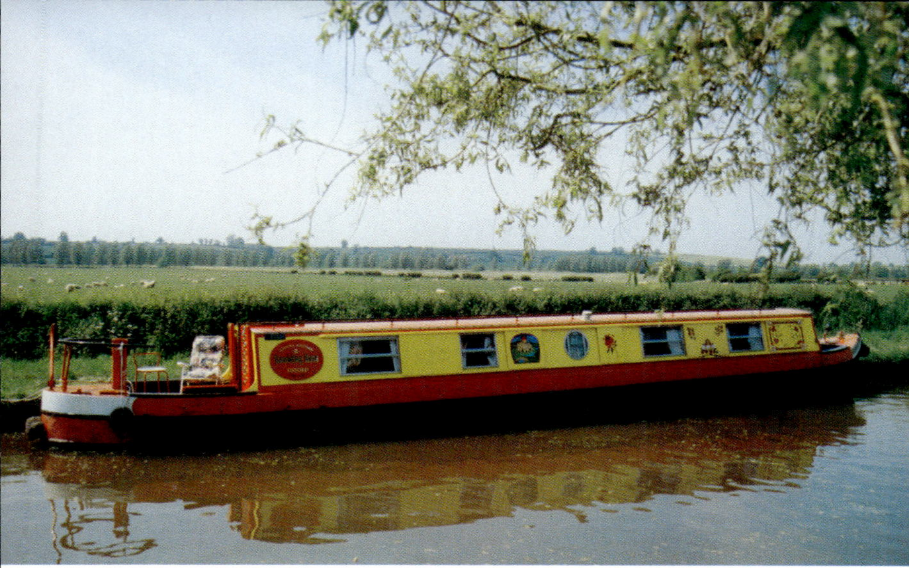

Don't just go for the obvious shot when taking photographs. This first picture of a canal boat is fine as a record shot, but lacks interest. Homing in with a telephoto lens for the second shot has revealed some interesting detail on the side of the barge.

Photograph: Philip Raby

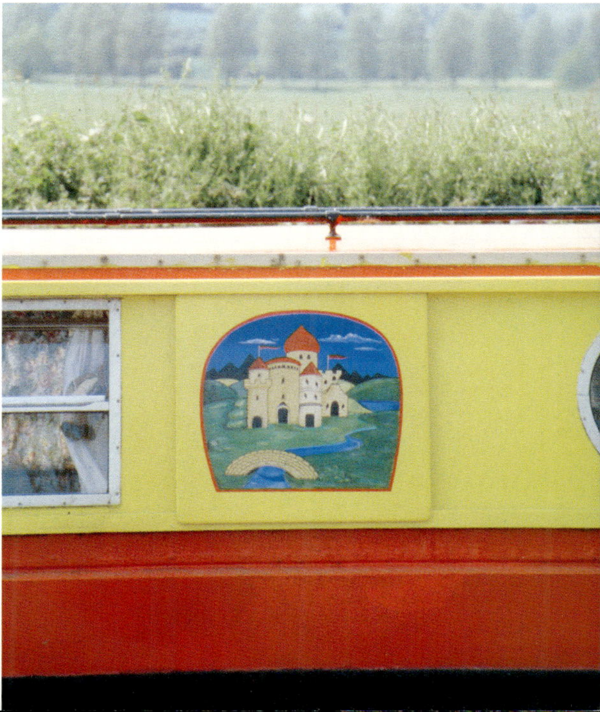

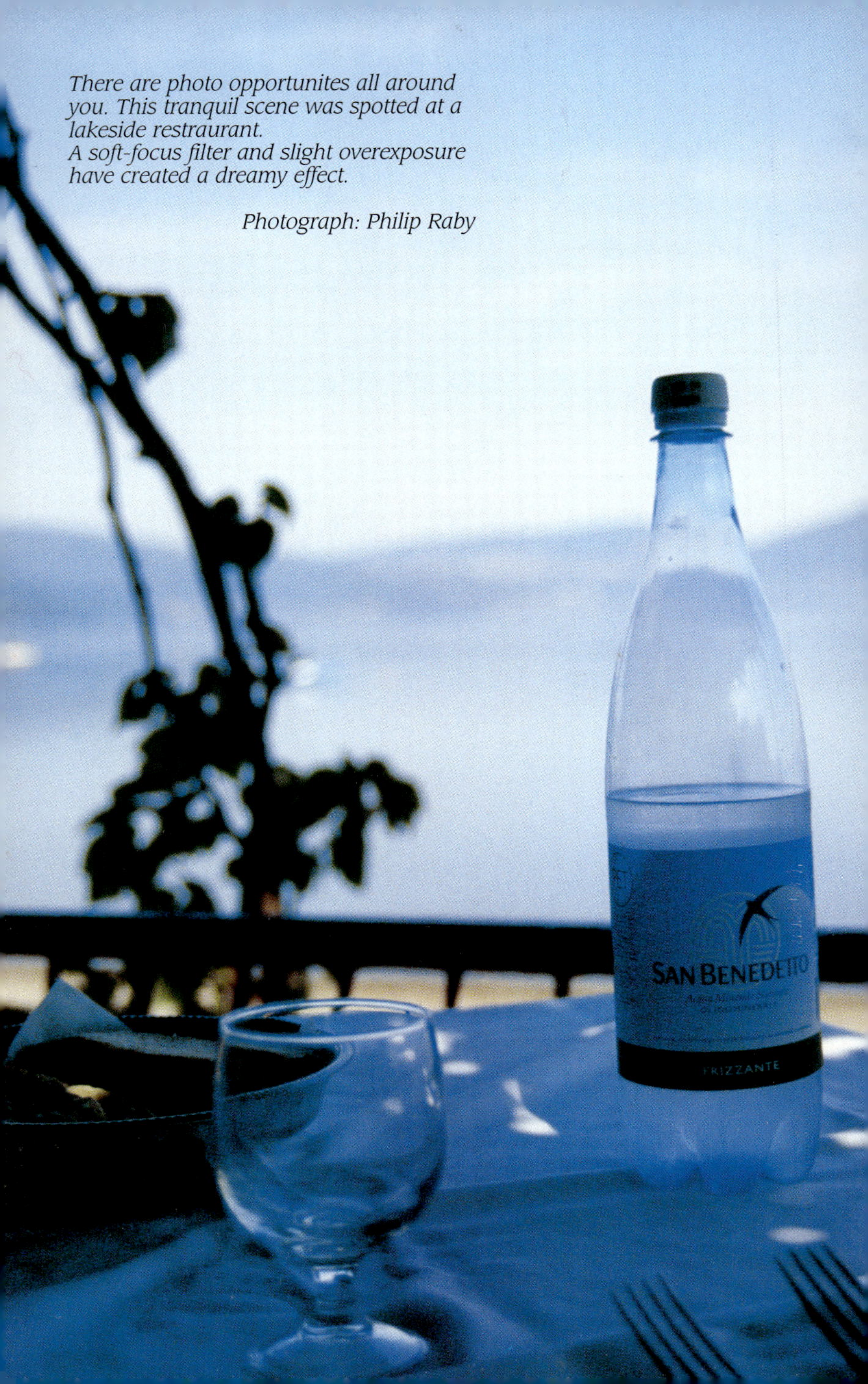

There are photo opportunites all around you. This tranquil scene was spotted at a lakeside restraurant.
A soft-focus filter and slight overexposure have created a dreamy effect.

Photograph: Philip Raby

Chapter 12

Basic flash photography

An essential ingredient for a successful photograph is light. The film in your camera reacts to light and forms a latent image. This image then becomes visible when the film is processed.

The EOS 300 – Rebel 2000 can still be used when the light drops. It has a small built-in flashgun that pops up from the top of the camera when it is needed. When you need more power, you can attach a dedicated Canon Speedlite to the camera. But don't think that flash can only be used in low light; later in this chapter we'll explain how flash can be used to improve your outdoor photographs.

If you have ever used flash with less sophisticated cameras you have probably been disappointed and frustrated by the results. Flash photography used to be a complex and often unreliable exercise. But the EOS 300 – Rebel 2000 with either its built-in flash or a Speedlite makes flash photograph straightforward and accurate.

This chapter explains briefly how to take flash photographs with your EOS 300 – Rebel 2000. If you have a Speedlite flashgun, you should also read the Hove Foto Books User's Guide to Canon Speedlites 420EZ, 430EZ, 540EZ and 550EX.

What is TTL flash metering?

TTL stands for Through-The-Lens. A sensor inside the camera reads the amount of flash light that enters the camera lens and quenches the flash when enough light has been received for a correct exposure.

Simpler flash systems use a sensor on the front of the flashgun. The advantage of a TTL system is that it automatically compensates for filters, flash diffusers and bounced flash.

The Speedlite 540EZ features A-TTL flash metering in some modes; the A stands for Advanced. This system relies on a small preflash to determine the flash-to-subject-distance. Once the camera knows this, it sets an aperture that ensures a correct flash exposure and a correct ambient exposure, at all shooting distances within the range of the flash. The actual power of the flash is determined at the moment of exposure by a flash meter that measures the amount of light reflecting off the film surface.

The Speedlite 380EX, when attached to the EOS 300 – Rebel 2000, boasts E-TTL flash metering. This is an improvement of A-TTL metering that uses the camera's Evaluative metering for the flash reading – E stands for Evaluative.

This system determines the flash exposure by giving a preflash a split-second before the exposure. At the same time, the camera measures the ambient light to ensure that both the ambient and flash exposures are correct and balanced. It also takes into account the active focus point and ensures that the part of the picture you are focusing on is correctly exposed.

The power of the flash is controlled not by its brightness, but by its duration – the longer the flash, the more powerful it is. The duration varies between 1/750 and 1/20,000 second, so all you will notice is that a long flash appears brighter than a short one.

At the end of the day, of course, you do not need to know how TTL flash metering works, just that it creates great pictures!

Using the built-in flash

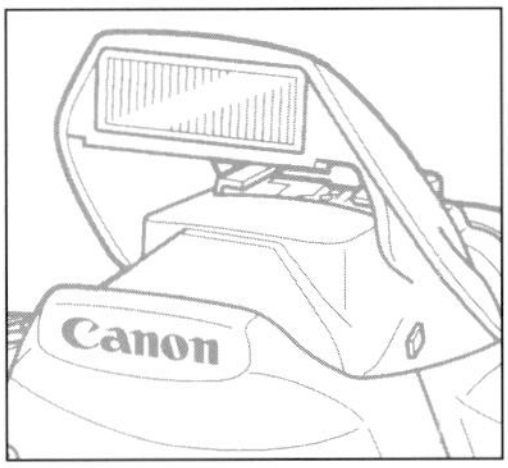

When your EOS 300 – Rebel 2000 is set to Full Auto, Portrait or Close-up mode, the built-in flash pops up when the camera senses that it is needed. This may be when it is dark, or if the camera senses strong backlighting. Either way, the camera uses TTL flash metering to ensure a correct exposure. This is the easiest way to take snapshots and other snatch photographs. The flash never fires in Landscape or Sport modes.

In Creative Zone modes, the built-in flash only fires when you want it to. To activate the unit, press the flash button which is located at the front of the camera just below the pentaprism.

The built-in flash has a coverage equivalent to the angle-of-view of a 28mm lens. If you use it with wider focal lengths, the edges of the image will not be illuminated. There is not a problem using the flash with focal lengths greater than 28mm.

Do not attach a lens hood when using the built-in flash – the hood may obstruct the light from the flash and cause part of the subject to be in shadow. For the same reason, Canon EF lenses with an extremely wide front element cannot be used with the built-in flash. These lenses include the EF 20-35mm f2.8L and most super-telephoto white lenses.

The built-in flash cannot be activated when an external flashgun is attached to the camera. Some people put a plastic cover over the camera hotshoe; don't do this, it is not necessary and will stop the flash from popping-up.

Light from a flashgun falls away with distance. Imagine driving on a dark night. Objects close to you are brightly lit by your car's headlamps, while those farther away remain in darkness until you get closer to them. The light from the built-in flash behaves in the same way. The range of the flash depends partly on film speed, but generally speaking, for successful built-in flash photographs, you should ensure that the subject is no farther than four metres from you.

Remember that using the built-in flash increases drain on the camera's batteries, so don't use it if the subject is a long way from you. You have probably seen flashguns firing at concerts, many metres from the performers. That is a waste of time; you either need to use a very fast film, or set a long shutter speed to ensure a good result in such situations.

The built-in flash can cause harsh shadows if the subject is in front of a wall. To avoid this happening, try to ensure your subject is some way in front of walls and other surfaces. Also, the direct flash can reflect off spectacles and windows. Ask your subject to take off their spectacles or look downwards. The easiest way to avoid reflections off windows is to close the curtains!

Don't be tempted to use flash for all your indoor photographs. If the room is attractively lit, the flash can destroy the ambience. If in doubt, take two photographs – one with flash and a second without.

Red-eye and the built-in flash

You have probably seen snapshots of people with glaring red eyes – a common problem with flash photographs. It is caused when bright light enters the eye – such as that from a direct flashgun – and is reflected off the blood vessels of the retina and coloured red by them. This leads to the distinctive red glow in the subject's eyes.

Red-eye is most likely to occur in dark conditions when the subject's pupils expand to let more light in. Children's pupils take longer to contract than adults and therefore are more susceptible to the problem.

Alcohol affects the reaction time of a person's pupils, which is one reason why red-eye often occurs on pictures taken at parties or down the pub!

Red-eye may also occur when you are photographing animals – especially nocturnal ones such as cats and foxes. These creatures have large pupils to enable them to see in dark conditions, which means that more light can enter and bounce off the retina. What's more, an animal's eyes may end up appearing green or yellow instead of red! This is because their retinas reflect light in a different way. You may have experienced this effect when driving along a dark road – animal eyes caught in the beam from your car's headlights develop a sinister glow.

The problem of red-eye occurs when the flashgun is close to the camera's lens axis. Therefore, the built-in flash is more likely to cause red-eye than a Speedlite, which is mounted farther from the lens.

You may think that red-eye only occurs with colour film. You'd be right, but don't think that you will automatically avoid the problem by shooting in black-and-white. Obviously the eyes won't appear red on a monochrome print, but they may reproduce pale and milky – which can look even more spooky than red-eye!

Red-eye reduction lamp

Your EOS 300 – Rebel 2000 has a red-eye reduction facility. This is a bright light that shines at the subject prior to the flash firing.

The light causes the subject's pupils to contract, limiting the amount of light that can enter the eyes and therefore reducing the risk of red-eye occurring.

Red-eye reduction works well so long as the subject is looking directly at the camera while the light is lit. And that can be a problem – people often look away when a bright light is shined at their eyes!

To set red-eye reduction, press the Function button on the top of the camera until the arrow in the LCD panel points to the red-eye reduction symbol appears. Then turn the Input Dial until '1' appears in the LCD panel.

To use red-eye reduction, activate the built-in flash and half press the shutter button; the red-eye reduction lamp will light and warning symbols appear in the LCD panel and viewfinder. After about two seconds, press the shutter button all the way to take the photograph. You can fire the shutter before two seconds is up, but the red-eye reduction lamp may not have had time to be effective.

Other ways of avoiding red-eye

Red-eye in photographs is caused by flash (although very occasionally it can occur with other bright lights, such as a car's headlamps). So turn off the built-in flash and the problem goes away.

Of course, there are times when you have to use flash – if there is no available light, you have no choice but to activate the built-in unit. But sometimes the ambient light can be very attractive and may give better results than a flashgun. Remember to keep an eye on the shutter speed and be ready to use a tripod or monopod if it drops below hand-holding levels.

Red-eye is most likely to occur when the subject is looking straight at the camera. So ask them to look away from you while you take a photograph.

Don't think that portraits need to have the person looking straight at the camera. Often, you can achieve a more attractive photograph if your subject is looking into the distance, reading a book, or perhaps engaged in a favourite hobby.

In dim conditions, your pupils expand to let more light enter the eye and enable you to see better. This also lets in more light from a flash, therefore increasing the risk of red-eye. So if you increase the room lighting, your subjects' pupils will contract very quickly, making red-eye less of a problem.

Load a fast film (such as ISO 400). This requires less exposure and therefore the flash output will be less.

Red-eye is particularly troublesome with the built-in flash because it is so close to the lens axis. Treat yourself to a Canon Speedlite and the problem will reduce considerably. Adding a Sto-Fen diffuser to the Speedlite will practically eliminate the risk of red-eye. It will also reduce harsh shadows and reflections during flash photography. Ask your local photo dealer for details.

These techniques will ensure that red-eye does not spoil your photographs. But what about pictures that you already have? Before you throw away all your red-eye shots, treat yourself to a red-eye retouching pen. You can buy one from a photo dealer. It is basically a fibre-tip pen containing a special green ink. By following carefully the instructions that come with the pen, you can retouch the eyes and restore your family and friends to normal human beings.

A red-eye retouching pen will save your existing prints, but in future, remember that prevention is better than cure!

Using a Speedlite

Any EZ, EX or EG Canon Speedlite can be used with your EOS 300 – Rebel 2000. These include; Speedlite 160E, Speedlite 200E, Speedlite 300EZ, Speedlite 420EZ, Speedlite 430EZ, Speedlite 540EZ, Speedlite 550EX, Speedlite 300EX and Speedlite 480EG. The Macro Ring Lite ML-3 can also be used for close-up photography.

Here is a brief specification and description of the currently available models:

Speedlite 200E

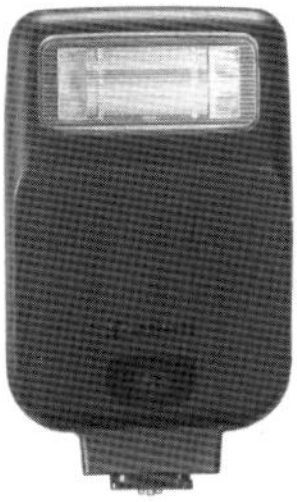

The Speedlite 200E is really designed for EOS cameras that do not have a built-in flash, so it is unlikely that you will want to buy one for your EOS 300 – Rebel 2000.

Like an EOS built-in flash, the low-power Speedlite 200E offers one mode – TTL, making it ideal for straightforward flash photography. Used with an Off Camera Cord, the Speedlite 200E is ideal for macro photography.

Specification

Type: Direct flash only
Modes: TTL (200M; external flash sensor only)
Focal length coverage: 35mm (28mm with clip-on adaptor)
Maximum Guide Number (ISO 100, m): 20
Power Source: 4x AA cells
Weight: 130g (excluding batteries)
Size: 64x104x41mm
Introduced: 1990

Speedlite 220EX

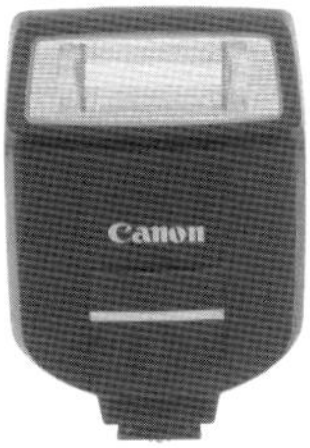

The Speedlite 220EX is a small, lightweight, simple-to-use E-TTL flashgun. It has a fixed forward-facing head and offers an FP mode which gives flash synchronisation at all shutter speeds.

Specification

Type: Direct
Modes: E-TTL, TTL, FE Lock
Focal length coverage: 28mm
Maximum Guide Number (ISO 100, m): 22
Power Source: 4x AA cells
Weight: 160g (excluding batteries)
Size: 65x92x61mm
Introduced: 1996

Speedlite 380EX

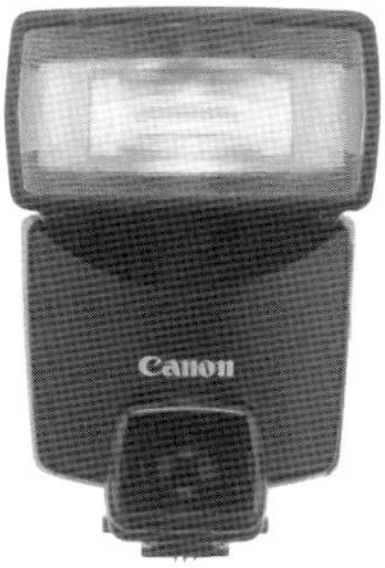

The Speedlite 380EX is designed especially for use with the EOS 300 – Rebel 2000, although it can also be used with other EOS models. When used with the EOS 300 – Rebel 2000, it offers E-TTL flash metering, flash synchronisation at all shutter speeds in FP mode and FE Lock. The head tilts upwards, but does not swivel from side to side.

Specification

Type: Bounce
Modes: E-TTL A-TTL, TTL FE Lock
Focal length coverage: 24-105mm, auto-zoom
Maximum Guide Number (ISO 100, m): 38
Power Source: 4x AA cells
Weight: 270g (excluding batteries)
Size: 80x138x112mm
Introduced: 1995

Speedlite 540EZ

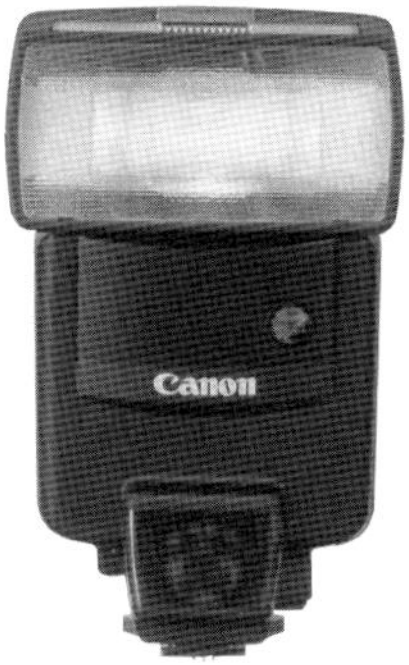

The Speedlite 540EZ is a top-of-the-range flashgun with a range of features, including fill-in ratio control; manual power settings from 1/1 to 1/128 power and strobe flash frequencies up to 100Hz.

To avoid the flash 'missing' the subject during close-up photography, the bounce head can be tilted down 7°.

Specification

Type: Bounce and Swivel
Modes: A-TTL, TTL, Variable power manual
Focal length coverage: 24-105mm, auto-zoom with manual override
Maximum Guide Number (ISO 100, m): 54
Power Source: 4x AA cells, or external pack
Weight: 415g (excluding batteries)
Size: 80x138x112mm
Introduced: 1994

Speedlite 550EX

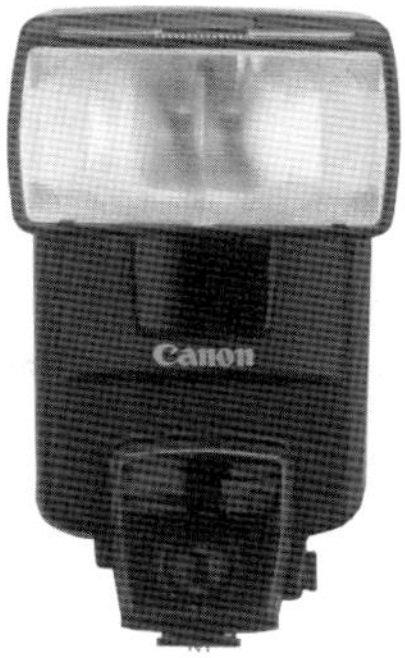

The Speedlite 550EX is similar to the Speedlite 540EZ, but has been updated especially for use with the EOS 300 – Rebel 2000 and so uses the latest E-TTL flash metering system. It is by far the best flashgun you can use with your EOS. It's also the first Speedlite to boast a wireless multiple flash system which allows a number of 550EX units to be used together without being linked by cables.

Specification

Type: Bounce and Swivel
Modes: E-TTL, TTL, Variable power manual
Focal length coverage: 24-105mm, auto-zoom with manual override
Maximum Guide Number (ISO 100, m): 55
Power Source: 4x AA cells, or external pack
Weight: 415g (excluding batteries)
Size: 80x138x112mm
Introduced: 1998

Speedlite 480EG

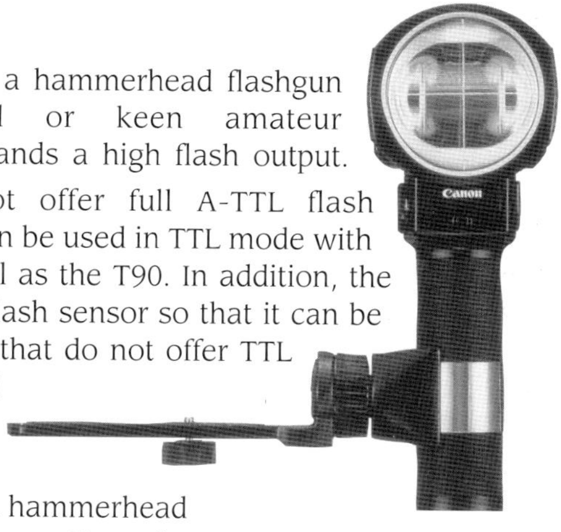

The Speedlite 480EG is a hammerhead flashgun for the professional or keen amateur photographer who demands a high flash output.

The 480EG does not offer full A-TTL flash metering. However, it can be used in TTL mode with all EOS cameras, as well as the T90. In addition, the 480EG has an external flash sensor so that it can be used with SLR cameras that do not offer TTL metering – the Canon F-1 or A-1, for example.

Specification

Type: Bounce and swivel hammerhead
Modes: TTL, External sensor, Manual
Focal length coverage: 35mm (20mm with Wide Panel, 135mm with Tele Panel)

Maximum Guide Number (ISO 100, m): 48
Power Source: Transistor Pack E or NiCad Pack TP
Weight: 715g (excluding batteries)
Size: 98x256.5x114.3mm (excluding bracket)
Introduced: 1993

Attaching a Speedlite

The hotshoe (sometimes called an accessory shoe) on top of your EOS 300 – Rebel 2000 is designed specifically to hold a Speedlite.

Not only does the hotshoe hold the Speedlite firmly in the optimum place for even flash coverage, it also has a number of electrical contacts. These link the camera and flash so that they work together as a single unit.

The Speedlite 220EX, Speedlite 380EX, Speedlite 430EZ, Speedlite 540EZ and Speedlite 550EX have a locking pin that engages with a hole in the camera hotshoe. This ensures that the flashgun is securely mounted and cannot slip off. Turn the locking ring on the base of the Speedlite clockwise to lock it onto the camera. Turn it anticlockwise to remove the Speedlite.

Once the Speedlite is attached and switched on it will fire for all your photographs.

See the next chapter for more information on using a Speedlite with your EOS 300 – Rebel 2000.

Macro Ring Lite ML-3

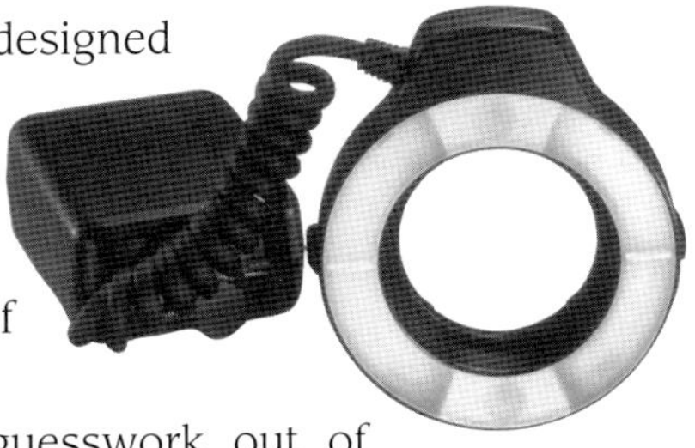

The Macro Ring Lite ML-3 is designed for close-up and macro photography. The flash unit mounts on the end of the lens and gives a ring of light to ensure even illumination of close subjects.

TTL metering takes the guesswork out of macro flash photography, which used to involve complex calculations to allow for the close focusing.

If you take macro photography seriously, the ML-3 is an essential addition to your EOS outfit.

Specification

Type: Macro ring flash
Modes: TTL
Focal length coverage: 50mm for macro, 28mm for normal
Maximum Guide Number (ISO 100, m): 11
Power Source: 4x AA cells
Weight: Control unit 235g (excluding batteries): Flash unit 115g
Size: Control unit: 74x60.5x106.5mm Flash unit: 101x120.5x20.6mm
Introduced: 1989

Chapter 13

Using flash

Flash in different shooting modes

Flash photography is possible in every shooting mode of your EOS 300 – Rebel 2000, but the results may be different in some modes to others. See Chapter 4 for information on flash in PIC modes.

Full Auto

In Full Auto mode, the built-in flash fires when the camera senses that it is needed. If a Speedlite is attached to your EOS 300 – Rebel 2000, it fires for every photograph, even if it not strictly required.

Program Mode

In Program mode, the built-in flash must be activated manually by pressing the flash button, The camera sets a shutter speed of 1/90 second. The aperture is chosen according to subject distance – as calculated by the preflash – and ambient light level. This ensures a correct balance of ambient and flash exposures, down to a light level of EV10. At lower light levels, the ambient exposure is ignored to ensure that long shutter speeds are not set.

Shutter Priority mode

When using Shutter Priority, the built-in flash must be activated manually by pressing the flash button. With either the built-in flash or a Speedlite you are limited to a shutter speed of 1/90 second – the flash sync speed. If a shutter speed faster than the sync speed is set before the flash is turned on, the camera automatically overrides it and set the sync speed.

The camera tries to set itself to give a correct exposure to the ambient light as well as the flash. If it is unable to do this, the viewfinder display will flash. You can ignore this and the flash exposure will be correct, but the background which is lit by daylight, might be underexposed.

The Speedlite 540EZ reverts to TTL mode when the camera is set to Shutter Priority mode.

Aperture Priority mode

You need to be careful using Aperture Priority mode with flash. The camera tries to ensure that the ambient exposure is correct, and as a result may end up setting a long shutter speed. You need to be aware of this and be ready to use a tripod if the shutter speed drops below hand-holding levels.

In bright light the camera may need to set a fast shutter speed to give a correct exposure, especially if you have chosen a wide aperture. However, when a Speedlite is attached, the camera is unable to set a speed faster than 1/90 second, in which case the picture may be overexposed. If this occurs, the shutter speed will flash in the viewfinder.

The Speedlite 540EZ reverts to TTL mode when the camera is set to Aperture Priority mode.

Manual mode

During flash photography, setting the camera to Manual makes a difference to the flash metering system of Speedlites – A-TTL or E-TTL is replaced by TTL metering.

This can be very useful because the flashgun no long emits a preflash, which is a nuisance to wildlife photographers who do not want to scare their subjects, or to photojournalists taking candid shots.

Because there is no preflash, the camera cannot calculate the subject distance. Instead, the Speedlite displays the range that the flash will cover for the aperture, film speed and focal length you are using. So, as long as you know roughly how far you are from the subject, and you keep within the suggested range, you will get correctly exposed flash pictures. If your subject is beyond the indicated range, try setting a wider aperture, this will increase the flash range.

Note that the flash range is only displayed when the flash head is pointing forward, the values would not apply to bounce flash.

In Manual mode, you can set any shutter speed, including Bulb, up to 1/90 second – the flash sync speed. If a faster shutter speed is set, this will be overridden when the flash is activated.

When your EOS 300 – Rebel 2000 is set to Manual it gives a guide to the ambient exposure in the viewfinder. You can use this to ensure that the background is correctly exposed, or ignore it and set a fast shutter speed and small aperture to give a dark background behind a subject correctly exposed by flash.

Auto Depth mode

Flash should not be used in A-Depth mode. If you try to use either the built-in flash or a Speedlite, the camera will revert to Program mode.

Chapter 14

Using your EOS with studio flash

If you have a home studio, or are a professional photographer or member of a camera club, there is a good chance that you will want to connect your EOS 300 – Rebel 2000 to studio flash units. These are large, powerful flash units mounted on stands. Unlike a Speedlite, studio flash units are manual only – they give out a fixed power flash and are not dedicated to the camera.

Although studio flash units do not have the sophistication of a Speedlite, they are more powerful. What's more, they feature modelling lamps. These are tungsten bulbs – rather like those in your home – that simulate the effect of the flash tube. In other words, the modelling lamps allow you to see what the lighting will look like so that you can make adjustments before firing the shutter – something that you cannot do with a Speedlite.

Studio flash units connect to the camera via a PC lead. No one is too sure what PC stands for. Some say it is short for Prontor Compur, the shutter manufacturers that designed the system. Others vote for Pin Cylinder, after the shape of the little plugs – the choice is yours. Either way, there is no denying that PC leads are a nuisance. The plugs are very small and not a positive fit. They date back to the days when flash leads plugged into a socket on the side of the lens where space was at a premium. The design became an almost universal standard, and today we are stuck with it.

Although the EOS 300 – Rebel 2000 does not have a PC socket you can still connect studio flash units, using an accessory called a hotshoe/PC adaptor – a little cube that fits onto the camera hotshoe and has a PC socket in the side. PC/Hotshoe adaptors are inexpensive, but also unreliable – they do not always form a good contact with the camera.

You can damage your camera by connecting an old-fashioned studio flash unit with a trigger voltage greater than 6v. However, modern equipment has a much lower trigger voltage and can be used quite safely.

Once you have done all this, there is a fair chance that the flash units will not fire when you press the shutter button! There are a number of reasons for this.

First, some types of studio flash, when used with Canon cameras, require a reverse polarity flash lead. This looks exactly the same as a normal flash lead, but the terminals on the plug are connected the other way around. Reverse polarity flash leads are available in the shops – Olympus OM cameras also use them. Or you can make your own – cut a normal PC lead, strip the wires and reconnect them the other way around.

Second, if the flash is not firing, try wiggling the adaptor around to see if you can make a contact.

Third, the flash lead may be too long. Leads longer than about 4 metres do not always work with EOS cameras. Also, multiple leads joined together can cause problems.

Last, the flash lead may be faulty! This is not uncommon. Most studios have a selection of leads, so try them one at a time.

If this all sounds like a lot of hassle – and it can be – there is an alternative. Most studio flash units have a slave cell. This is a light sensitive sensor that is triggered by the flash from another flashgun. All you have do is fit a Speedlite onto your camera, set it to low-power Manual, and bounce it off a wall or ceiling. The Speedlite will fire when you press the shutter, and activate the studio units. You may need to experiment with the angle of the Speedlite and the power setting. Remember that it is giving out a very low power flash compared to the studio units, and therefore will have little effect on the final photograph. And if you wonder if the studio flashes will fire quick enough to synchronise with the camera shutter, just think how fast light travels!

Setting the camera

Once you have connected your flash units, you must set your EOS 300 – Rebel 2000 to Manual – you cannot use any other mode. You can use any shutter speed up to 1/90 second – the sync speed of the camera. Unlike using a Speedlite or built-in flash, when a non-dedicated flash unit is attached, the camera does not override shutter speeds faster than the sync speed – it is up to you to ensure that a suitable speed is set.

Aperture must be determined by a hand-held flash meter. Check that the meter is set to the correct film speed before taking a reading.

Chapter 15

Self-timer operation

The self-timer feature of your EOS 300 – Rebel 2000 puts a ten second delay between the shutter button being fully pressed and the shutter actually firing. The main use for this is for you to be able to include yourself in your photographs – handy for group shots that you want to be part of and times when you don't have anyone to take your photograph for you. However, the self-timer also has another use, as we shall find out.

Setting the self-timer

To set your EOS 300 – Rebel 2000 to self-timer mode, all you have to do is press the self-timer button on the top plate (Diagram 32). The self-timer symbol will appear in the LCD panel. Now when the shutter button is depressed there will be a ten second delay before the shutter fires. You have four minutes after setting self-timer mode to press the shutter button; after this the camera reverts to normal operation.

To cancel self-timer mode, press the self-timer button again.

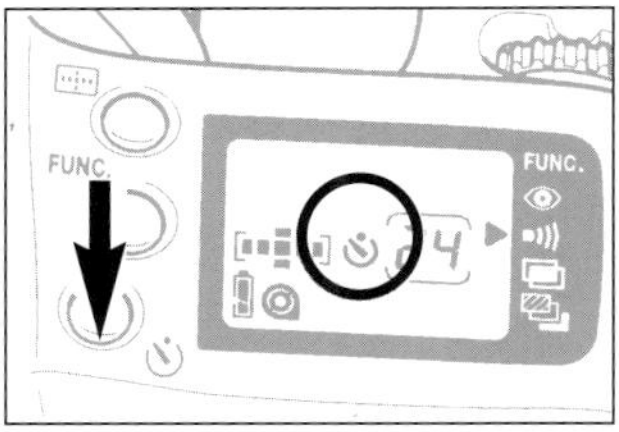

Diagram 32:

Press the Self Timer button on the top of the camera to set it to self-timer mode.

Using the self-timer

Any shooting mode can be used for self-timer photography. After setting self-timer mode, and within four minutes, press the shutter button halfway to focus and take an exposure reading. Now press the shutter button fully. The Red-eye Reduction light will flash and the camera will beep at 2Hz (twice a second) for eight seconds. During the last two seconds, the beeping and flashing increase to 8Hz (eight times a second) to warn you that shutter firing is imminent – time to smile!

Focusing

When taking a self-portrait, there is a risk that the camera will focus on the background and you will be out of focus. To avoid this happening, either get someone to stand in your place while you focus, or switch the lens to Manual focus and prefocus on the point where you will be standing. If there is enough light, set a small aperture so that there is plenty of depth-of-field to compensate for any slight focusing error.

Use a tripod

When using the self-timer, the camera must be firmly supported, ideally on a sturdy tripod; no you can't use a monopod! If you do not have a tripod handy, use a portable clamp, or place the camera top of a wall, chair or table – look in the viewfinder to make sure that the surface does not appear in the picture. Make sure that the camera is safely supported – you don't want to see it toppling to the floor just before the shutter fires!

Eyepiece cover

Look at the strap that came with your EOS 300 – Rebel 2000. It's got a piece of plastic threaded onto it (diagram 33). This is a viewfinder cover for self-timer operation.

This is necessary because, when your eye is not up to the camera, there is a slight risk that light will enter the viewfinder and affect the exposure reading. The eyepiece cover avoids this happening.

To use the eyepiece cover, first remove the rubber eyecup. You can then slide on the eyepiece cover – the cover remains on the strap.

For most of your self-timer photographs it is unlikely that stray light entering the viewfinder will adversely effect the exposure. However, if there is bright light shining directly into the viewfinder then it is a good idea to use the eyepiece cover.

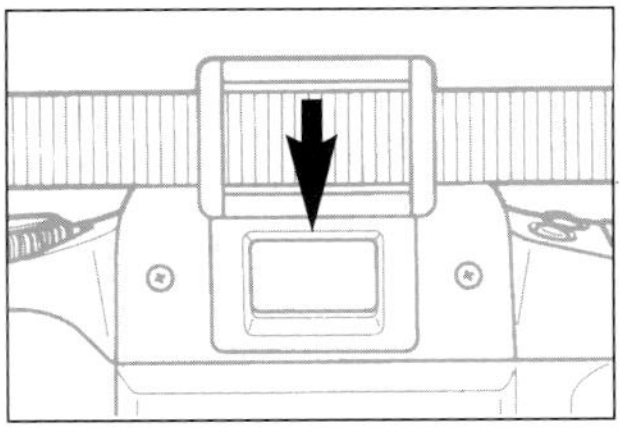

Diagram 33:

Part of the strap doubles as an eyepiece cover.

Use the self-timer to avoid camera shake

At the beginning of this chapter it was hinted that the self-timer was not just for taking self portraits. It can also help you avoid camera shake spoiling your photographs.

Even when the camera is mounted on a sturdy tripod, the act of pressing the shutter button can cause the camera to move slightly. At normal shutter speeds, this is not a problem, but during long exposures it can cause the image to be blurred.

One solution is to use a remote control (see Chapter 18), but if you do not have one handy, set the self-timer. The ten second delay is long enough for any movement caused by pressing the shutter button to subside.

This technique works well for inanimate objects, but is not suitable for moving subjects or situations when you need to fire the shutter at a precise moment.

Chapter 16

Quartz Date models

The EOS 300 – Rebel 2000 is available with a Quartz Date back that prints the date or time onto the film as you take a photograph. These models are designated 'QD'.

Unlike some EOS models, you cannot add the Quartz Date back to a normal EOS 300 – Rebel 2000, so when you buy your camera, think carefully whether or not you have a need for data imprinting, if you think you do, then go for the Quartz Date version.

How the Quartz Date back works

Inside the Quartz Date back is a tiny numerical Light Emitting Diode (LED) display behind the film pressure plate. This shines through the film onto the light sensitive emulsion where it causes a latent image to form. The colour of the LED display is such that the image on the processed film is orange, to stand out against most subjects. The data appears in the bottom right-hand corner of horizontal format photographs.

The Quartz Date back includes an electronic clock and calendar that ensure that the information printed on the film is accurate and you can see exactly when you took each photograph.

Setting the Quartz Date back

Before using the Quartz Date back, you must set it to the correct time and date. The procedure for this will be familiar to anyone who has set a digital watch or clock.

First, press the Mode button to display either the time or the date, depending on which you wish to set. Then press the Select button, a section of the read-out will flash. Press the Select button until the part of the read-out that you wish to alter flashes. Now press the Set button continuously until the correct reading appears. Press the Select button to store that setting and move on to the next part of the read-out. When the read-out is correct, press the Select button until the flashing stops.

From time to time, check that the time and date are correct. If you travel to another time zone you need to decide whether to reset the clock, or leave it on your home time zone.

Using the Quartz Date Back

By pressing the Mode button you can select five data imprinting options:

- -- -- -- Data imprinting off (nothing printed onto film)
- 5 29 99 Date as month, day, year (May 29 1999)
- 29 5 99 Date as day, month, year (29 May 1999)
- 99 5 29 Date as year, month, day (1999 May 29)
- 29 14 30 Day and date as Day, hour minute (29th 2.30pm)

If you wish to use date imprinting, choose a format that you understand and always use the same one.

Having the data printed on all your pictures can be annoying, so remember to turn off the feature when you do not require it – always check to see if data imprinting is on before you start shooting. Some people just imprint the date onto the first frame of each film, or at the start of the day, that is often enough to help you to keep a shooting record.

When you are using data imprinting, bear in mind that the information is going to be in the bottom right corner of each horizontal photograph, and in either the top right or bottom left of vertical pictures, depending on which way you hold the camera. A solution is to move back slightly to leave a border around your picture that can be cropped out afterwards. Alternatively, take two versions of the picture – one with data imprinting and a second without.

Replacing the Quartz Date back battery

The Quartz Date back has its own power supply that powers the clock and calendar. This lasts about three years, after which the LCD panel on the back will start to fade.

To replace the battery, first check that you do not have a film loaded. Open the camera back and look at the inside of it by the hinge. You will see an arrow pointing at a little silver screw. Use a tiny screwdriver to remove this screw and the battery compartment lid will come loose. Remove it and hook the battery out. Put in a fresh battery and replace the cover. Finally put back and tighten the little screw. If you are not confident about doing this, take the camera to your local Canon dealer for help.

The time and date must be reset after replacing the battery.

Chapter 17

Canon EF lenses

Until recently, most SLR cameras were sold with what is known as a standard 50mm lens. The idea was that the lens had a similar angle-of-view to the human eye. In fact, most of us have an angle-of-view which is closer to a 35mm lens, but a 50mm lens was useful for general photography.

In recent years, the quality of zoom lenses has improved to such an extent that the 50mm lens has been replaced by the standard zoom lens – one with a range that includes the 50mm setting. You probably bought your EOS 300 – Rebel 2000 with an EF 28-80mm f3.5-5.6 III USM.

Although a standard zoom is an ideal first lens and copes with most picture-taking situations, there will come a time when you want to add to your lens armoury. Maybe you want to get closer to distant objects, or include more in the frame. Before looking at the options available, let's find out more about Canon EF lenses.

Why buy a Canon lens?

Lenses that will fit onto your EOS 300 – Rebel 2000 are made, not only by Canon, but also by independent lens manufacturers. Although some of these are very good, others are not. Canon has a reputation to maintain so all of its lenses offer excellent optical quality.

Most of today's Canon EF lenses boast Ultrasonic focus motors, although other manufacturers have tried to copy this system, there is no doubt that the original is fastest, quietest and best.

If you buy a Canon lens you can be sure that it will be fully compatible, not only with your EOS 300 – Rebel 2000, but also with future EOS models. There have been compatibility problems with some independent lenses.

Although an independent lens may be cheaper to buy, don't

forget that its resale value is likely to be much less than a comparable Canon optic. Canon lenses always command good second-hand prices.

Lens motors

Your EOS 300 – Rebel 2000 has a built-in autofocus system. This sends signals to a motor in the lens that drives the lens elements in and out until the image is in focus. When autofocus cameras were in their infancy, most manufacturers chose to put the focus motor in the camera body. This meant that you did not have to buy a lens with each motor, but there had to be a mechanical link between the camera and lens.

Canon's engineers were not happy with this concept, they wanted a totally electronic lens mount without any moving parts that could go wrong. What's more, a mechanical linkage absorbs energy and makes focusing slower and less accurate. Another reason that Canon rejected the camera body lens motor system is that different lenses require different power motors. A wide-angle lens is lighter and has less distance to travel than does a super-telephoto lens. Canon's system means that each lens can be fitted with the optimum motor.

Early Canon EF lenses use Arc Form Drive, or AFD, motors. This works in the same way as conventional electric motors but, as its names suggests, it is in the shape of an arc so that it follows the contours of the lens barrel. AFD motors make a slight noise as they focus the lens, but for most people this sound is not obtrusive.

Some Canon lenses still use AFD motors, but most now feature the almost silent Ultrasonic motor, or USM. These lenses are identified by the initials 'USM' after the lens description, and also by an 'Ultrasonic' logo on the side of the barrel. Unlike ordinary electric motors, USMs use ultrasonic vibrations from piezoelectric elements. These vibrations cause the motor to rotate.

Not only are USM lenses silent, they are also faster than AFD powered optics.

Some popular Canon lenses use a Micro USM drive, also called

Micro Motor, or MM. These offer the same performance as conventional USMs , but are more compact.

One or two low-cost Canon EF lenses feature a simple DC motor that is slower and noisier that a USM, but quite adequate as an entry-level lens.

All Canon EF lenses contain a second motor, this drives the aperture diaphragm. It is a stepping motor, which means that each time it receives an electric pulse from the camera, it moves one step. So by sending a number of pulses, the camera can control exactly how far the motor travels, and therefore accurately set the aperture.

The diaphragm motor is activated as you press the shutter button to take a photograph, so that the aperture is stopped down to the predetermined amount. It is also used to stop down the aperture during depth-of-field preview.

Focal length

The focal length of a lens is an important part of its description. It is defined as the distance between the rear nodal point of the lens and the film plane, when the lens is set to infinity, and is expressed in millimetres. But don't worry, you don't have to get a tape measure out to find out focal length – just look at the words around the front element. A short focal length, such as 28mm has a wider angle-of-view than does a long focal length lens, such as 200mm. A long focal length lens makes distant objects appear closer, while a short focal length takes in more of a scene.

Maximum aperture

Also written on the front of every Canon EF lens is an aperture value. This is the maximum aperture of the lens. Chose a lens with a wide maximum aperture, for instance f1.8, for low light photography. You may hear people refer to a wide maximum aperture lens as fast, this is because it allows you to set a faster shutter speed than would be possible with a smaller maximum aperture lens in the same conditions. Fast lenses tend to have large front elements to allow more light to enter. They are also more expensive than slower lenses.

Some zoom lenses have a variable maximum aperture that depends on the focal length set. For instance, most standard zooms have a maximum aperture that varies from f3.5 to f5.6.

Prime and zoom lenses

Once upon a time, all lenses had a fixed focal length. Then along came zoom lenses with variable focal lengths. However, the optical quality of these early zooms left a lot to be desired and were spurned by serious photographers.

Today, zoom lenses give excellent results and are used extensively by amateurs and professional photographers alike. But they do have their drawbacks. The main one being that in most cases they do not offer such a wide maximum aperture as an equivalent fixed focal length, or prime, lens. For instance, a standard zoom lens normally has a maximum aperture range of f3.5-f5.6, while a cheap and cheerful 50mm prime lens has a maximum aperture of f1.8. If you want the ultimate standard lens, choose the incredible EF 50mm f1.0L USM lens, the world's fastest SLR camera lens.

Prime lenses still offer the best quality, but most people are unlikely to notice the difference between a picture shot on a Canon zoom and an equivalent prime lens.

Zoom lenses offer the advantage of being a number of lenses in one – an important consideration if you are planning on carrying your equipment over long distances. For most people, the convenience and versatility of zoom lenses make them the obvious choice.

L Series lenses

You will come across some Canon EF lenses with the suffix 'L' after their description. These L Series lenses offer super-high quality optics – at a price. If you demand the best, chose L Series lenses, but normal Canon EF lenses also offer excellent results.

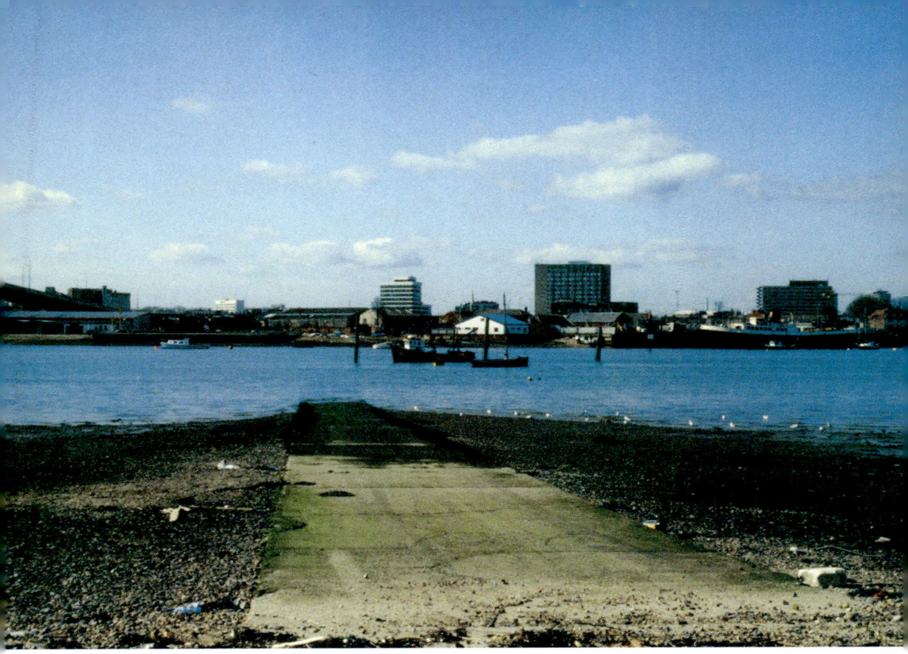

These two photographs were taken from exactly the same spot with the same tripod-mounted EOS, yet look totally different. The reason is that the first picture was taken with a so-called standard 50mm lens, whereas the second was shot with a 600mm telephoto.

Photograph: Philip Raby

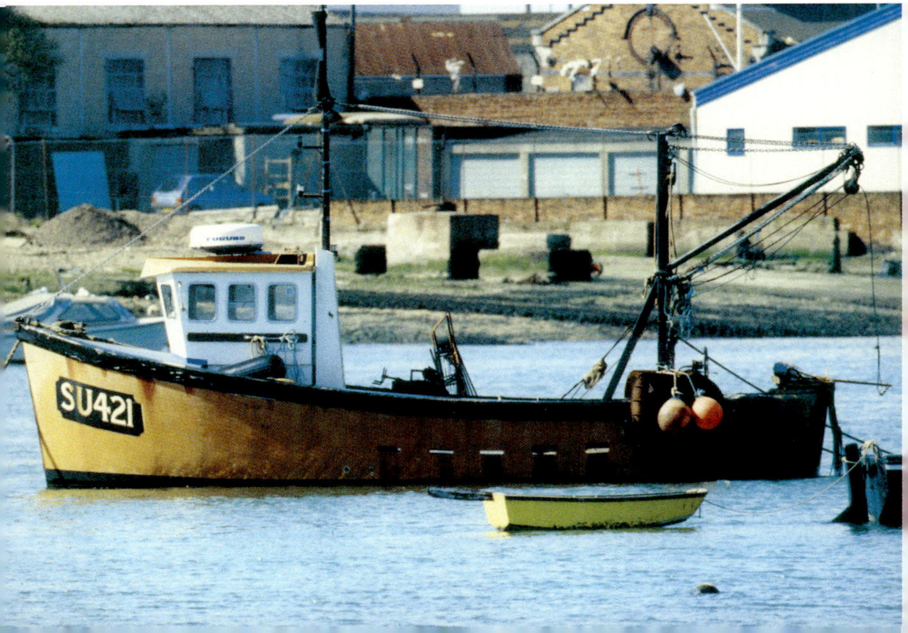

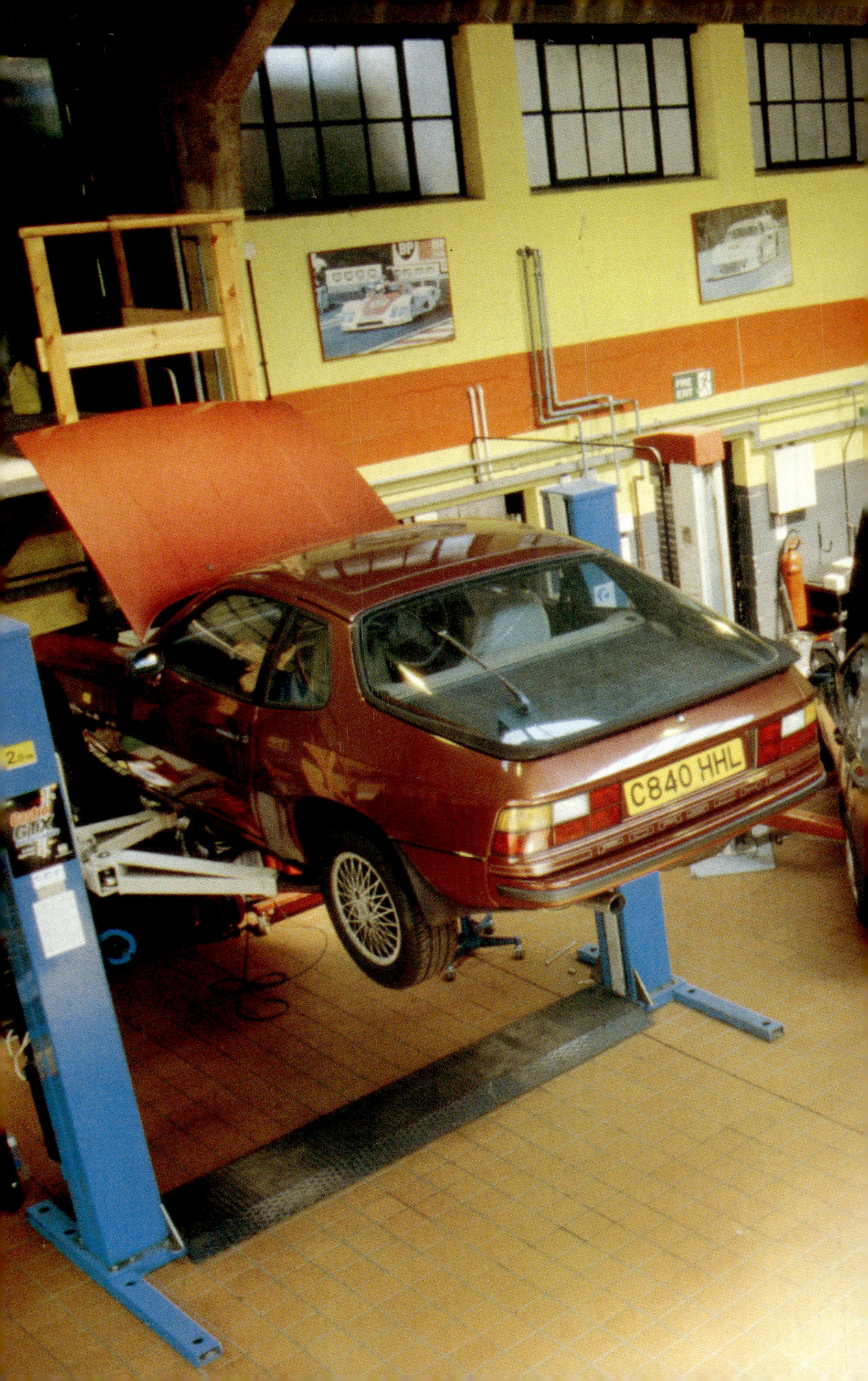
C840 HHL

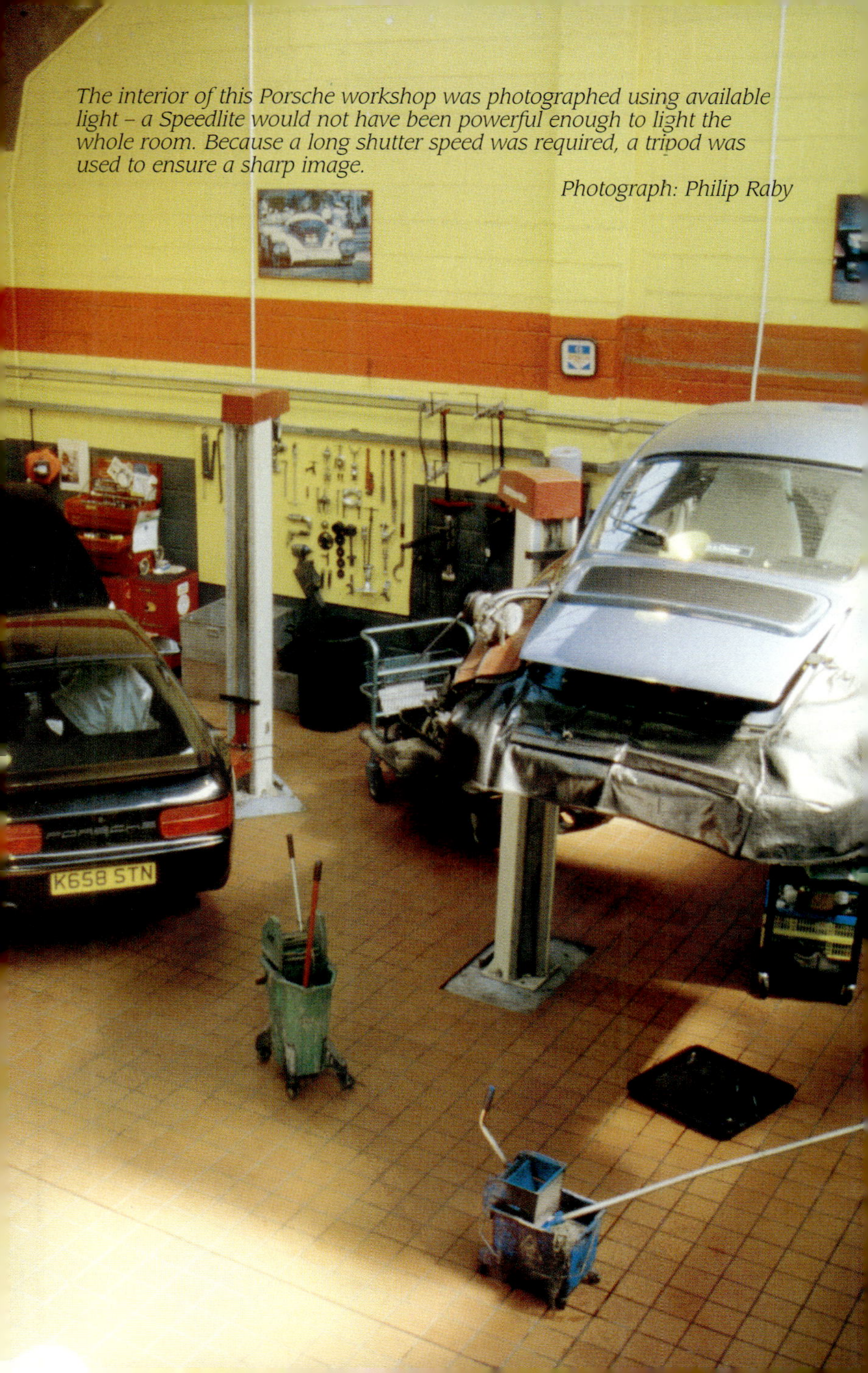

The interior of this Porsche workshop was photographed using available light – a Speedlite would not have been powerful enough to light the whole room. Because a long shutter speed was required, a tripod was used to ensure a sharp image.

Photograph: Philip Raby

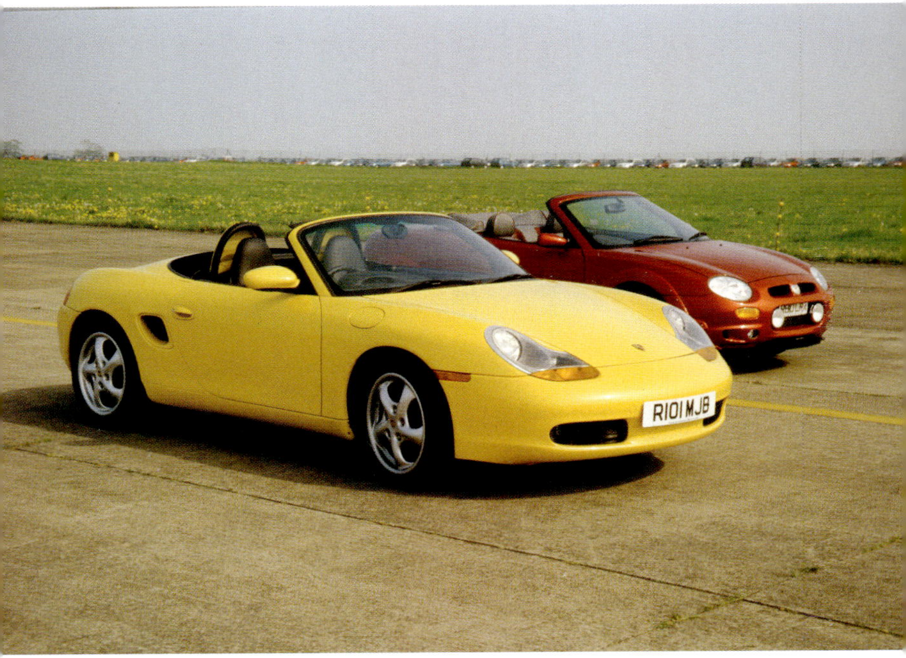

This Porsche Boxster and MGF were photographed with a standard zoom lens at the wide-angle setting to give a dramatic effect.

Photograph: Philip Raby

Wide-angle prime lenses

A wide-angle lenses are those with a focal length wide than 50mm. They take in more of a scene with their wide-angle-of-view, but objects appear small and distant in the viewfinder. What's more, wide-angle lenses can create great depth-of-field, making them ideal for landscape photography. Here are just some Canon EF wide-angle prime lenses.

EF 14mm f2.8L USM

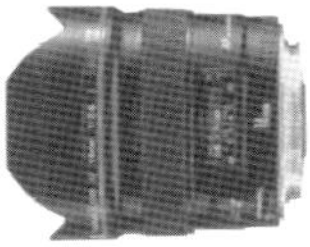

This lens has an angle-of-view of 114°, but it is has rectilinear characteristics. This means that, unlike a fish-eye lens, it does not distort straight lines, but offers a more natural effect. This lens is ideal for photographing interiors and other situations where space is at a premium.

EF 15mm f2.8 Fisheye

Although there is only 1mm difference between this lens and the EF 14mm f2.8L USM, it actually has a wider angle-of-view – an incredible 180°. It distorts straight lines around the edge of the frame to create an exciting and distinctive fisheye effect.

The angle-of-view of this lens is so extreme that you have to be careful that you do not include your feet in photographs! You should also be aware of tripod legs and other unwanted paraphernalia.

Think carefully before buying the EF 15mm f2.8 Fisheye lens. The extreme effects it produces have limited uses; you may be better getting the more conservative EF 14mm f2.8L USM. Some camera dealers offer a hire service so you could rent this lens when you have a specific need for it.

EF 24mm f2.8

This is a very useful lens. Its angle-of-view of 84° is not too extreme, making it suitable for general photography, but the lens can still produce exciting wide-angle effects when you want it to.

EF 28mm f1.8 USM

Although only 4mm between this and the EF 24mm f2.8, this lens has quite different qualities. It is an ideal first wide-angle lens because of its subtle characteristics and almost natural perspective. It also has an unusually wide maximum aperture, making it useful for low light work.

EF 35mm f2

Here's a lens with a similar angle-of-view to the human eye, making it many people's choice of a 'standard' lens, instead of the more traditional 50mm focal length. It gives a very natural perspective and is useful for landscapes, group shots and interiors.

Standard lenses

As mentioned earlier, SLR cameras were once mostly sold with a 50mm standard lens. Although zoom lenses have almost taken their place, standard lenses still have their uses. Let's take a look at some.

EF 50mm f1.8 II

A superb lens for very little money. This lens is small, light and compact, yet boasts a wide maximum aperture and excellent optical quality.

EF 50mm f1.4 USM

An alternative to the EF 50mm f1.8 II with a wider maximum aperture and Ultrasonic focus motor for fast, quiet operation.

EF 50mm f1.0L USM

A specialist lens that can be identified by its huge front element, necessary for the incredible maximum aperture of f1.0. This is the world's fastest SLR camera lens and is seven times the weight of the humble EF 50mm f1.8 II. Who said 50mm lenses were dull?

Short telephoto lenses

Lenses with focal lengths of around 100mm are often known as portrait lenses because they are ideal for taking pictures of people. Their focal length is long enough to give yourself enough distance from the subject not to intimidate them. What's more, when used at a wide aperture, these lenses throw backgrounds out-of-focus, drawing attention to the subject. Here are a few Canon short telephotos.

EF 85mm f1.2L USM

You may wonder what the point of this lens is when its focal length is covered by standard zooms. But look at that maximum aperture of f1.2 – not only is that useful for low light photography, it also allows you to reduce depth-of-field to a minimum.

EF 135mm f2.8 SF

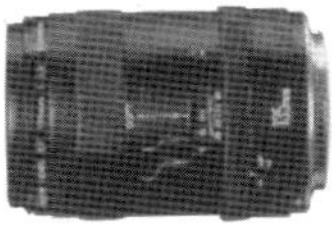

Here's a lens that will appeal to the keen portrait photographer. Its focal length is ideal for taking pictures of people, and the wide maximum aperture throws backgrounds out-of-focus. What's more, it features a useful soft focus facility.

Soft focus does not mean out-of-focus, but the image is softened by carefully controlled flare. The lens has a switch on its side that allows you to set one of two levels of soft focus. The '1' setting gives a subtle effect, while '2' is more extreme.

The amount of soft focus also depends on lens aperture. A wide aperture setting increases the soft focus effect, while small aperture reduce it considerably.

When you don't want the soft focus effect, you can turn it off and you are left with a superb short telephoto lens that gives pin-sharp images.

Medium telephoto lenses

When you cannot get close enough to your subject, you need a longer focal length lens. These medium telephotos are not so long that they have to be mounted on a tripod (although you should use a tripod or monopod whenever possible), yet are powerful enough to fill the frame with distant subjects.

EF 200mm f2.8L USM

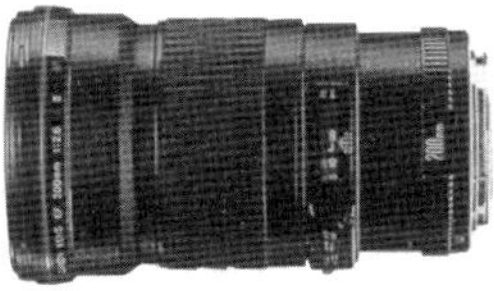

200mm is a very useful focal length to have in your lens collection. This lens is light enough to hand hold and has a wide maximum aperture for low light work.

EF 300mm f4L USM

If you require a bit more pulling power, the extra focal length of this lens is useful. It is a low-cost lens and therefore only has a maximum aperture of f4. At focal lengths greater than 200mm you really should be using a tripod whenever possible.

EF 300mm f2.8L

This is a lens for professionals. It's expensive, but gives superb results and allows you to set a wide aperture to maintain a high shutter speed - essential for sports photography.

Super-telephoto lenses

When you start looking at lenses with focal lengths greater than 300mm, you're getting into the range of exotica - specialist lenses for specialist applications. Choose one of these if you are a keen sports or wildlife photographer. If you only need a long focal length occasionally, you may be better off hiring a lens when you require one.

EF 400mm f5.6L USM

This is the lowest priced super-telephoto lens. Compared with faster lenses, it is light and compact.

EF 400mm f2.8L USM

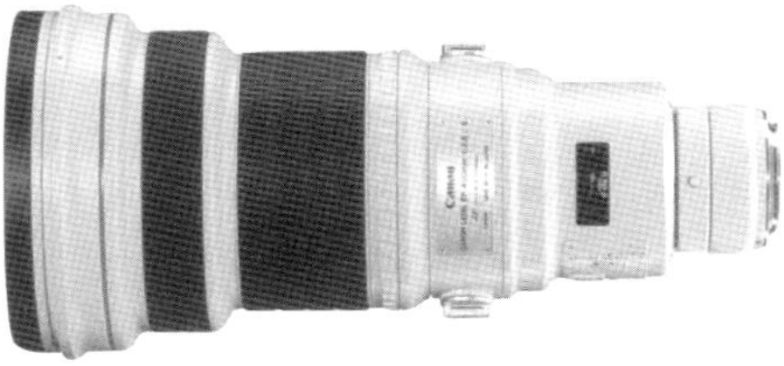

Here's a super-telephoto with a super-wide aperture. It's big and expensive, but ideal for sports photographers who need to be able to set wide apertures to keep shutter speeds high. The wide aperture combined with the long focal length also means that depth-of-field can be reduced to a minimum.

EF 500mm f4.5L USM

Despite its focal length, this lens is surprisingly light and compact, making it ideal for wildlife photographers who have to carry their equipment over long distances.

EF 600mm f4L USM

This is a beast of a lens – big, expensive, and heavy. But the results from it can be incredible. A favourite lens amongst sports photographers.

EF 1200mm f5.6L USM

Here's a lens you are unlikely to buy. It costs about the same as a small house or a very nice Porsche 911 Carrera. And at 16.5kg, hand-held photography is definitely out! The lens has an angle-of-view of just 2° and its closest focusing distance is 14 metres.

1200mm not enough for you? Fit the Extender EF 2x for a super-super-telephoto of 2400mm!

If you should win the lottery, don't go to you local dealer for this lens – it is only made to special order.

Wide-angle and standard zoom lenses

As mentioned earlier, your EOS 3 probably came with a with an EF 28-80mm f3.5-5.6 III USM, a standard zoom lens that covers the most frequently used focal lengths. Here are some other wide and standard zooms.

EF 20-35mm f2.8L

This is a useful alternative to a prime wide-angle lens. It has a wide maximum aperture and a range of angle-of-views from 80° to 54°. what's more, it gives superb results at all focal lengths. An expensive lens, but worth every penny.

EF 28-80mm f2.8-4L USM

A luxury version of the standard zoom, this lens gives super-high quality results and has the benefit of a wide maximum aperture.

EF 28-105mm f3.5-4.5 USM

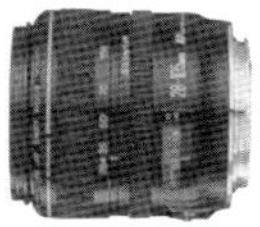

The extra range of this lens makes it worth considering as a standard zoom instead of the EF 28-80mm f3.5-5.6 III USM. At the 105mm end, it is a useful portrait lens.

Telephoto zoom lenses

A telephoto zoom lens is probably the first lens you will buy to accompany your standard zoom. Let's take a look at a few from the Canon arsenal.

80-200mm f4.5-5.6 USM

A useful lens with a focal length range that follows on neatly from that of the standard zoom. This lens is superb value for money and surprisingly compact at just 78mm long.

EF 100-300mm f4.5-5.6 USM

A zoom lens with a very useful range. But remember that at focal lengths greater than 200mm, a tripod is almost essential for pin-sharp photographs.

EF 75-300mm f4-5.6 USM

A lower-cost alternative to the EF 100-300 f4.5-5.6 USM. A compact, lightweight lens with a superb focal length range.

EF 35-350mm f3.5-5.6L USM

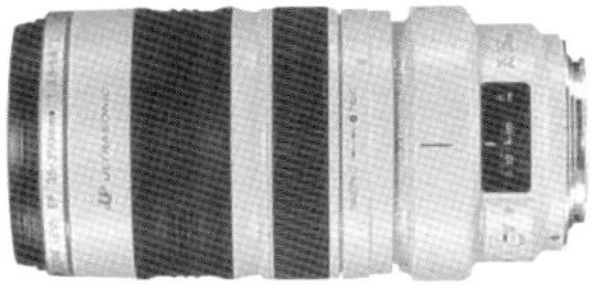

The ultimate zoom lens, this covers most focal lengths that you will ever need. Just think, no more carrying a bag full of lenses around with you, and no missing a vital shot because you have the wrong lens on your camera. The EF 35-350mm f3.5-5.6L is not cheap, but it could be more economical than buying a number of lenses.

This lens is not designed to be used with Canon Extenders, but it can be attached to an Extender and gives good results. However, autofocus may not operate at all focal lengths.

Image stabilization lenses

Your EOS 3 looks after focusing and exposure, so the main cause of failed photographs is camera shake. Canon offers unique Image Stabilization lenses which address the problem.

Inside an Image Stabilization lens are two sensors that measure the amount of camera shake. This information is fed to a 16-bit microprocessor that converts the signals into drive commands for the Image-Stabilization mechanism. This is a series of coils and magnets that move a floating group of lens elements to compensate for camera shake and ensure that a steady image reaches the film.

A switch on the side of the lens allows you to switch Image Stabilization on or off. In the off position, the lens acts like any other. Image Stabilization should be turned off when the camera is used on a tripod or in the Bulb setting.

Image Stabilization does not eliminate the effect of camera shake, but it does reduce it considerably. The rule-of-thumb for hand-held photography is that the shutter speed should be no less than the inverse of the shutter speed. So if your focal length is 200mm, the shutter speed should be no longer than 1/200 second. Image Stabilization allows you to reduce this safe shutter speed by up to two stops and still get similar results.

Here are some Canon Image Stabilization lenses, all are based on standard optics from the Canon stable but with the IS mechanism added:

EF 75-300mm f4.5-5.6 IS USM

This was the first Canon IS lens and took the world by storm. It is a sensibly priced lens with a useful focal length range.

EF 28-135mm f3.5-5.6 IS USM

You may wonder why you'd need IS on a wide-angle lens, but this versatile optic is designed as a standard zoom which can be kept on your camera at all times, increasing the chances of sharp photographs, even in low light. This is well worth considering as your standard lens.

EF 100-400mm f4.5-5.6L IS USM

A useful lens that gives you a range of focal lengths from short to long telephoto, and all with the benefit of IS, allowing you to take handheld photographs even at 400mm. The L suffix guarantees the ultimate in image quality, too.

The EF 100-400mm f4.5-5.6L IS USM is a superb lens with the added benefit of Canon's unique Image Stabilization system.

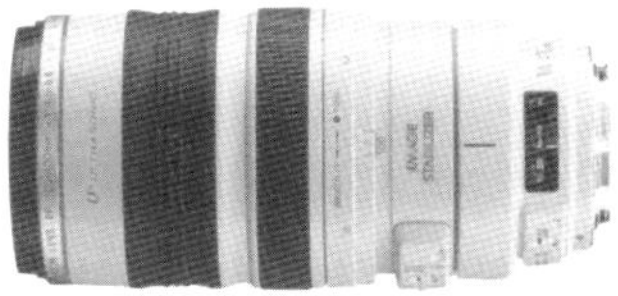

EF 300mm f4.0L IS USM

This telephoto lens can be used with Canon Extenders, giving a range of IS-equipped focal lengths. It offers two IS modes – '1' for general use and '2' for panning shots. The reason for the second mode is that if you're moving the camera sideways to track a subject, IS would try to counteract that movement. The Panning mode switches off IS in the horizontal plane, while retaining it for up and down shake.

Tilt-and-shift lenses

The axis of most cameras lenses is at right-angles and central to the film plane, to ensure that the image is in focus and free from distortion. However, Canon produces three special lenses that have barrels that can be shifted up down, or sideways in relation to the film plane, and also tilted in any direction.

These movements allow you to control perspective, for instance to photograph a tall building without it appearing to be toppling over. They also give the facility to control depth-of-field and much more.

Canon TS-E lenses do not have focus motors – you must focus them manually. However, this is not normally a problem – tilt-and-shift photography takes time to set up, so you are unlikely to need to focus quickly.

TS-E 24mm f3.5L

A wide-angle tilt-and-shift lens for architectural and interior photography. Its wide angle-of-view can create dramatic images.

TS-E 45mm f2.8

Probably the most useful tilt-and-shift lens. Its angle-of-view gives a natural perspective, making the lens useful for architectural, still-life and other general photographic situations.

TS-E 90mm f2.8

The long focal length of this lens makes it less suitable for architectural photography – you are unlikely to be able to get far enough from most buildings to include them in the frame. However, it is an ideal lens for still-life photography because it gives a useful working distance between the camera and subject and allows you to control depth-of-field and perspective. It can also be used with Life Size Converter EF for macro photography.

Macro lenses

Macro photography opens up a whole new world. This special macro lenses allow you to get in close to your subject and still maintain sharp focus. They can also be used as conventional lenses.

EF 50mm f2.5 Compact Macro

A standard 50mm lens that focuses down to 23cm to give half life-size images. It can be fitted with Life Size Converter EF to give life-size images.

EF 100mm f2.8 Macro

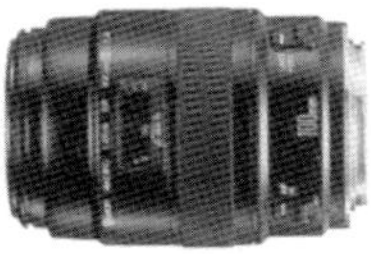

A superb lens that gives life-size macro images at its closest focusing distance of 31cm. The longer focal length means that there is a greater working distance between the camera and subject, which means that you are less likely to scare off insects and small animals. It also makes it easier to light the subject.

The EF 100mm f2.8 is also a useful short telephoto lens that is ideal for portraiture.

EF 180mm f3.5L Macro USM

A macro lens with a long focal length to give maximum working distance between the camera and subject for ease of lighting. The closest focus distance is 48cm with life-size magnification. It doubles as a superb telephoto lens for conventional photography.

Chapter 18

Accessories for your EOS 300 - Rebel 2000

Your EOS 300 – Rebel 2000 and standard zoom lens is a self-contained picture-taking machine that can cope with a wide range of photographic situations. However, a range of accessories is available to help you get even more from your camera. Here are just some of these.

Battery Pack BP-200

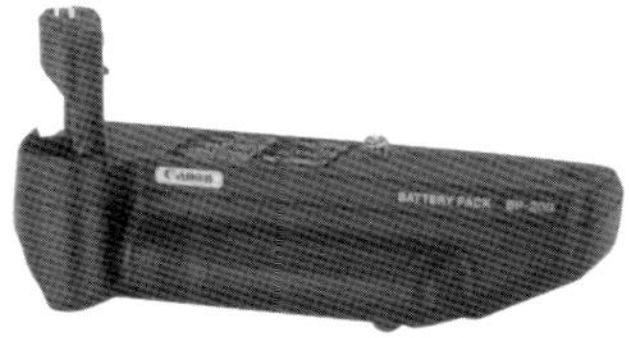

Your EOS 300 – Rebel 2000 is normally powered by a pair of compact, highly efficient lithium cells that fit in the camera's hand-grip. Although this is an ideal power supply in most situations, the batteries can normally only be bought from specialist photo and electronics dealers. You won't find one in a remote country store on a Sunday morning!

Far more readily available are AA-size pen cells, as used in radios, torches, toys and Speedlite flashguns. Battery Pack BP-200 allows you to power your EOS 300 – Rebel 2000 with these versatile little cells.

The pack fits neatly onto the base of the camera and is attached via the tripod socket (there is an additional socket on the base of the pack so that you can still use the camera on a tripod). The camera's batteries must first be removed.

As well as ordinary disposable alkaline batteries, you can also load Battery Pack BP-200 with rechargeable NiCad cells to save money and protect the environment. High power lithium AA batteries should not be used – their high initial voltage may damage the camera's electronics.

Not only does Battery Pack BP-200 give you an alternative choice of batteries, it also acts as a vertical holding grip. Many photographers have difficulty using their camera vertically, which is why you see so few upright, or portrait, format pictures. Battery

Pack BP-200 makes the camera more comfortable to use vertically and has an auxiliary shutter button on its end so that you don't have to contort your finger around the top of the camera.

Battery Pack BP-200 will also appeal to photographers with large hands who want to make their camera a bit larger.

Remote Switch RS-60E3

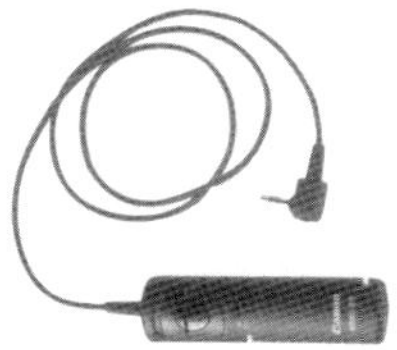

When your EOS 300 – Rebel 2000 is mounted on a tripod during long exposures there is a risk that it will move as you press the shutter button to take a photograph. This movement is called camera shake and may lead to a blurred picture. One solution is to attach Remote Switch RS-60E3. This plugs into the jack socket on the right-hand end of the camera. Its 60cm lead terminates in a small hand control that has button that duplicates the action of the camera shutter button.

Note that some other Canon EOS remote devices use a different type of plug and therefore cannot be used with the EOS 300 – Rebel 2000.

Lens accessories

Here are some accessories that allow you to do more with your Canon EF lenses.

Extension Tubes

An extension tube fits between the camera and lens to increase the lens-to-film distance and therefore allow closer focusing for macro work. Two extension tubes are available for your EOS 300 – Rebel 2000: Extension Tube EF25 which is 25mm long, and the shorter Extension Tube EF12 which is 12mm long.

Extenders

If you have an EF 70-200mm F2.8L lens or any EF telephoto prime lens with a focal length of 200mm or greater, you can use an EF Extender to increase the focal length of your lens, but with some reduction of maximum aperture.

Extender EF 1.4x increases the focal length by 1.4x and reduces the maximum aperture by 1 stop.

Extender EF 2x doubles the focal length but decreases the aperture by 2 stops.

An Extender can be used with the EF 35-350mm f3.5-5.6L USM, but autofocus may not be possible at all focal lengths.

Close-up lenses

These inexpensive accessories fit onto the front of your EF lens in the same way as a filter. In fact, they are often incorrectly called 'close-up filters' but they do not filter the light in any way.

What a close-up lens does is act like a magnifying glass, allowing you to focus much closer then normal and fill the frame with small objects. Because it does not reduce the amount of light that reaches the film, a close-up lens is an ideal introduction to macro photography.

Canon produces three close-up lenses – 500, 250D and 500D. Close-up Lens 500 is a low-cost item, but it still gives very good results. Close-up Lenses 250D and 500D have a double element design and offer higher image quality.

Lens hoods

One of the simplest and cheapest ways that you can improve your photographs is to use a lens hood. Canon produces lens hoods for most of its EF lenses and your photo dealer will be able to supply the correct one for your lens.

A lens hood reduces stray light from falling on the surface of the lens. This light is non image-forming and will cause flare that in turn degrades the image.

Dioptric Correction Lenses

Very few people have perfect eyesight, most of us are either short-sighted or long-sighted to some degree. However, the viewfinder of your EOS 300 – Rebel 2000 is calibrated for people with good eyesight. You may find that you can use the camera happily with your spectacles on, but some people find this awkward. It all depends on your particular eyes and the shape of your spectacles.

If you have trouble using spectacles with your camera, you can fit a correction lens to your EOS 300 – Rebel 2000. A range of correction lenses is available with their strengths indicated in dioptres, from -4 dioptres to +3 dioptres. The positive strengths are for long-sightedness and the minus ones for short-sighted people.

Remember to remove your spectacles when using an EOS with a Dioptric Correction Lens attached.

Camera Case EH13-L

A few years ago, everyone had an 'every-ready' case for their SLR camera. But they were not convenient to use and fell out of favour, being christened 'never-ready cases'!

However, Canon produces one for those photographers that like to keep their EOS 300 – Rebel 2000 protected. Camera Case EH13-L accepts the camera with an EF 28-80mm f3.5-5.6 III USM or EF 28-105mm f3.5-4.5 USM lens attached.

Chapter 19

Jargon buster – a glossary of EOS terms

If you thought that Fill-in Ratio control was something to do with plastering, and a PC lead was a non-racist, non-sexist contact, then you'd better read this glossary of EOS terms.

A-TTL

See Advanced TTL

Accessory shoe

See hotshoe

Advanced TTL

Normally called A-TTL. A through-the-lens (TTL) flash metering system unique to EOS cameras and Speedlites. It allows the camera and flash to work together to calculate the best shutter speed and aperture for a correct flash and daylight exposure.

AEB

See Auto Exposure Bracketing.

AFD

Short for Arc Form Drive, a focusing motor used in early Canon EF lenses.

AI Servo

A focus mode that continually tracks moving subjects.

Aperture

An adjustable hole formed by the lens diaphragm to limit the amount of light that reaches the lens.

Aperture Priority mode

A shooting mode that allows the photographer to choose the lens aperture.

Auto Depth mode

A shooting mode that allows the photographer to define how much of the image appears sharp.

Auto Exposure Bracketing

A feature of the EOS 300 – Rebel 2000 that allows you to take three photographs each at a slightly different exposure.

Auxiliary Focusing Light

A light on the front of the EOS 300 – Rebel 2000 and some Speedlites to aid focusing in low light.

BASIS

Short for Base Stored Image Sensor, part of the EOS 300 – Rebel 2000 autofocus system.

Battery

The power cells that provide the EOS 300 – Rebel 2000 with electricity. The standard batteries are two CR2 units, although readily-available AA batteries can be fitted in an optional external pack.

Built-in flash

The pop-up flash unit of the EOS 300 – Rebel 2000.

Bulb

A shutter speed setting available in Manual. When this is set, the shutter remains open as long as the shutter button is held down.

Canon

Manufacturer of cameras, lenses and accessories. Derived from the Buddhist name, Kwannon, it was changed to Canon in 1935 to avoid offending religious groups, and to sound more acceptable to Western ears. Both names are pronounced the same by the Japanese.

Centre-weighted Average metering

A metering system that takes a light reading from the whole image, but with an emphasis on the central area.

Close-up mode

A PIC mode for photographing near objects.

Command Dial

The dial on the top of the EOS 300 – Rebel 2000 that allows the shooting mode to be set. Also locks the camera when not in use.

Continuous

A winding mode of the EOS 300 – Rebel 2000 that allows a number of frames to be shot while the shutter button is held down.

Depth-of-field preview

A facility on the EOS 300 – Rebel 2000 that allows the aperture to be closed down prior to firing the shutter to see the amount of depth-of-field.

Dioptric correction lens

An optional lens that fits over the viewfinder that corrects for eyesight deficiencies. A range of different strength lenses is available.

DX Coding

A system of coding used on most 35mm film cassettes. The EOS 300 – Rebel 2000 reads this code to enable the correct film speed to be set.

EF lens mount

The lens mount used by the EOS 300 – Rebel 2000 and all other EOS models.

Input Dial

A rotary dial by the shutter button of the EOS 300 – Rebel 2000. Used to set camera functions such as shutter speed and aperture.

EOS

The name of Canon autofocus SLR cameras. Short for Electro Optical System and pronounced as one word – ee-os, not E.O.S.

Evaluative metering

The standard metering system of the EOS 300 – Rebel 2000. The scene is divided into segments and light readings taken from each section to ensure correct exposure in difficult lighting situations.

Evaluative TTL

Normally called E-TTL. A flash metering mode used by the EOS 300 – Rebel 2000 and EX-series Speedlites that utilises the camera's Evaluative metering system.

Exposure Compensation

A feature of the EOS 300 – Rebel 2000 that allows the exposure to be increased or decreased by a chosen amount.

Fill-in Ratio Control

See Flash Exposure Compensation.

First curtain sync

The standard way that a Speedlite or built-in flash is synchronised to the camera shutter. The flash fires immediately the shutter is fully open.

Flash Exposure Compensation
A feature on some Speedlites that allows the balance of the ambient and flash exposures to be altered.

Focal plane
The film plane inside the camera. The EOS 300 – Rebel 2000 uses focal plane shutter – it is directly in front of the film.

Focusing screen
Also known as a viewing screen. An opaque plastic screen inside the EOS 300 – Rebel 2000 that light is deflected onto from the lens to form an image.

Focusing ring
A knurled ring found on some EF lenses to allow manual focusing ring when the lens is set to Manual focus.

Full Auto
A simple-to-use shooting mode that turns the EOS 300 – Rebel 2000 into a point-and-shoot camera.

Function button
A button on the top of the EOS 300 – Rebel 2000 that sets certain camera features.

Guide Number
An indication of the power of a flashgun. By dividing by the flash-to-subject distance, it is possible to calculate the aperture to set for a correct exposure during manual flash photography. Can be quoted in either feet or metres and normally assumes the use of ISO 100 film.

Hotshoe
Fitting on top of the EOS 300 – Rebel 2000 that accepts a Speedlite or other accessories. It has electrical contacts that electronically link the camera and flash.

Landscape mode

A PIC mode for photographing scenery.

Liquid crystal display (LCD)

An electronic device that becomes black when an electronic charge is passed through it. The LCD panel on the EOS 300 – Rebel 2000 displays information about camera settings.

Lock

A setting on the EOS 300 – Rebel 2000 that turns off the camera and prevents the shutter from firing.

Macro Ring Lite

A Canon ring flash that attaches to the front of the lens and gives even illumination for macro photography. Often incorrectly called Macro Lite.

Manual mode

A shooting mode that leaves the photographer to set both the aperture and the shutter speed.

Multiple exposures

A feature of the EOS 300 – Rebel 2000 that allows more than one exposure to be made on a single frame of film.

Night Scene

A PIC mode that combines flash with a long shutter speed to ensure that background detail is recorded.

Off camera flash

A technique using a flashgun not mounted on the camera hotshoe.

Off Camera Shoe Cord

A Canon accessory that allows a single Speedlite to be used a short distance away from the EOS 300 – Rebel 2000 while retaining all dedicated functions.

One shot

A focus mode of the EOS 300 – Rebel 2000 that focuses once and then locks the focus setting.

Op/Tech

The world's most comfortable camera strap.

Partial metering

A metering system that takes a light reading just from the central 9.5% of the image area.

PC lead

A simple two-core lead used to connect a camera to a non-dedicated flashgun.

PC/hotshoe adaptor

Allows a PC lead to be connected to the EOS 300 – Rebel 2000, which does not have a PC socket.

PIC modes

See Program Image Control.

Portrait mode

A PIC mode for photographing people.

Program Image Control

Commonly known as PIC modes, these are easy-to-use setting that customise the EOS 300 – Rebel 2000 to suit specific photographic subjects.

Program mode

A shooting mode where the camera sets both the shutter speed and the aperture, but the photograph can override some settings.

Program Shift

A feature that allows the photographer to alter the settings made by the EOS 300 – Rebel 2000 in Program mode while retaining a correct exposure.

Quartz Date (QD)

A version of the EOS 300 – Rebel 2000 with a facility for the time or date to be imprinted onto the film.

Red-eye reduction

A light shone at the subject by the EOS 300 – Rebel 2000 during built-in flash photography. It helps to reduce the risk of red-eye – a distinctive effect caused by light from a direct flash entering a subject's eyes and bouncing off red blood vessels behind the retina.

Reflex mirror

A mirror inside the EOS 300 – Rebel 2000 that deflects light that has passed through the lens onto the focusing screen.

Remote control

An accessory that allows you to control the EOS 300 – Rebel 2000 from a distance. Also used to avoid camera shake.

Second curtain sync

A setting on some Speedlites that causes the flash to fire just before the shutter closes, instead of immediately the shutter is fully open.

Self-timer

A setting on the EOS 300 – Rebel 2000 that delays the firing of the shutter for ten seconds after pressing the shutter button.

Shutter

A blind in the camera that opens for a preset time to allow light to reach the film.

Shutter button

This button is pressed to take a photograph.

Shutter Priority mode

A shooting mode that allows the photographer to choose the shutter speed.

Single

A winding mode of the EOS 300 – Rebel 2000 that takes one photograph each time that the shutter button is pressed.

SLR

Short for Single Lens Reflex, the EOS 300 – Rebel 2000 is an SLR camera. A mirror and prism deflect light passing through the lens to the focusing screen so that what you see in the viewfinder is the same image that the film is exposed to when the shutter button is pressed.

Speedlite

The brand-name of Canon electronic flashguns.

Sport mode

A PIC mode for photographing action.

Sto-Fen

An aftermarket flash diffuser to reduce the risk of red-eye, harsh shadows and reflections during flash photography with a Speedlite.

Stop-down metering

The metering system found on the EOS 300 – Rebel 2000 that allows non-dedicated lenses and accessories to be used.

Sync speed

The maximum shutter speed that can be used for flash photography on a camera with a focal plane shutter. The sync speed of the EOS 300 – Rebel 2000 is 1/125 second.

Through-the-lens

See TTL metering.

TTL metering

Short for through-the-lens. A meter inside the camera body measures light that has passed through the lens.

USM

Short for Ultrasonic Motor, a fast, silent focusing motor used in Canon EF lenses.

Viewfinder

The eyepiece at the back of the EOS 300 – Rebel 2000 that you look through to see the image.

Chapter 20

Specifications

Viewfinder coverage: 90% horizontal and vertical.

Focusing screen: New Laser-matte screen, non-interchangeable.

Shutter: Electronically controlled vertical-travel focal plane shutter.

Shutter speeds: 1/2000 to 30 seconds plus Bulb. Can be set in 1/2 step increments.

X sync: 1/90 second (flash sync at all speeds when using Speedlite with HP mode).

AF control system: TTL-SIR (Through-The-Lens Secondary Image Registration) phase-detection type using BASIS (Base Stored Image Sensor).

AF modes: One-shot AF, AI Servo with Predictive AF, AI Focus (switches automatically between One Shot and AI Servo). Manual focus possible.

Focusing points: Seven points provided. Can be set by camera or user.

AF working range: EV 1-18 at ISO 100.

Light metering: TTL full aperture metering using a 35-zone SPC (Silicon Photo Cell). Three metering patterns available: Evaluative metering; Centre-weighted Average metering; Partial metering (approx. 9.5% of image area) at centre of screen.

Metering range: EV 2 to 20.

Film speed range: ISO 6 to 6400 (set by user); ISO 25 to 5000 (set by DX).

Shooting modes: Full Auto; Portrait; Landscape; Close-up, Sports; Night Scene; Shutter Priority AE; Aperture Priority AE; Automatic Depth-of-Field AE; Intelligent Program AE; E-TTL, A-TTL and TTL Program Flash AE; Manual; Bulb.

Exposure compensation: ±2 stops in 1/2 step increments.

Auto Exposure Bracketing (AEB): ±2 stops in 1/2 step increments.

Multiple exposure: up to 9 can be preset.

Depth-of-field preview: Possible.

Film loading: Automatic.

Film wind: Automatic Pre-wind system; Single or Continuous exposure.

Maximum winding speed: approximately 1.5 fps.

Film rewind: Automatic. Mid-roll rewind possible.

Power source: Two CR2 lithium cells. Optional Battery Pack BP-200 available.

Built-in flash: Guide number 12 (ISO 100, metres).

Flash contacts: Hotshoe.

Remote control: 2.5mm jack socket.

Self-timer: 10 second delay.

Size: 140 x 90 x 58.5mm.

Weight: 335g.

Introduced: August 1999.

ACCESSORIES WELL WORTH LOOKING AT!

OP/TECH

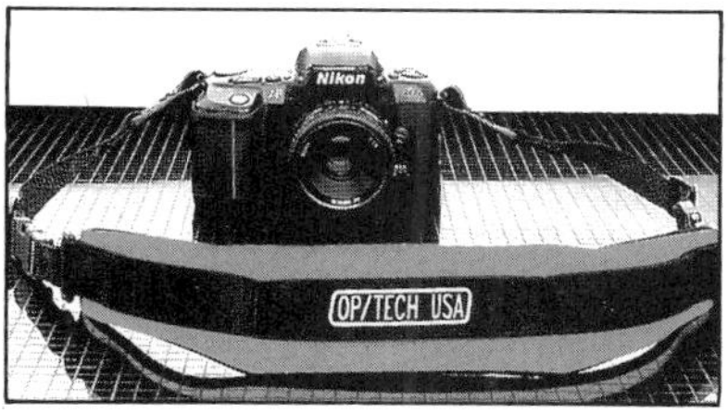

The world's most comfortable cameras, bag and tripod straps (binoculars too). Op/tech has a built-in weight reduction system that makes equipment feel 50% lighter and 100% more comfortable. From the famous 'Pro-Camera Strap' to the 'Bag Strap' and the 'Tripod Strap', the style, colours and comfort which along with the non-slip grip, ensure that you have a wonderful combination of comfort and safety.

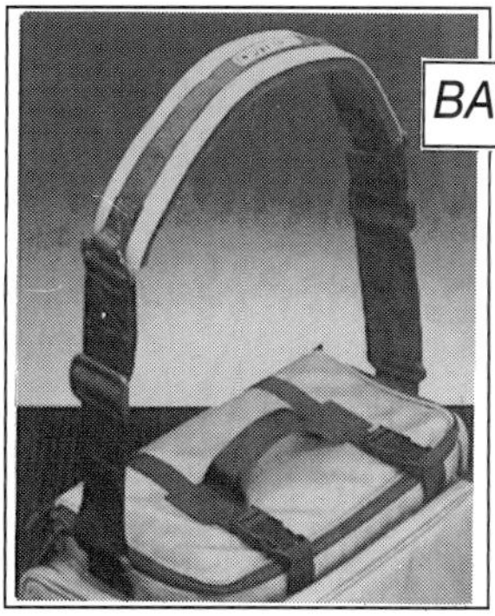

BAG STRAP

The **OP/TECH USA Bag Strap** is the answer to the problem of carrying a heavy bag for extended periods of time. By combining the patented weight reduction system with the Non Slip Grip™, you have the perfect strap for camera/video bags and cases as well as garment bags. Adjustable from 29" to 52", this strap is one of a kind. You will feel the difference!

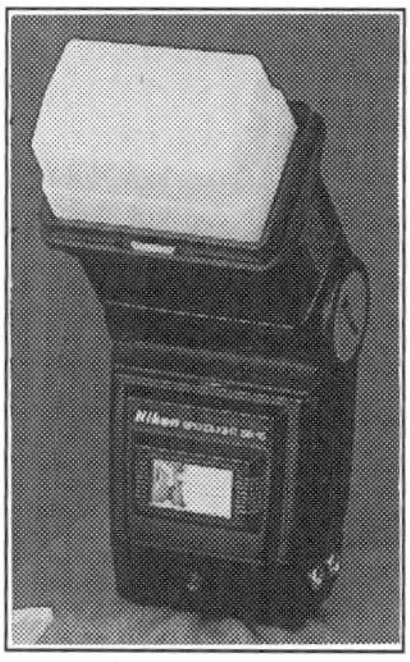

STO-FEN

The ultimate lightweight diffuser system for high powered modern flashguns. Sto-Fen offers the 'Omni-Bounce' for overall soft diffusion – often called the "softie" – which weighs in at just 15 grams and the 'Two-Way' Bounce Card for those who prefer to direct diffused light from their flash. The 'Two-Way' only weighs 25 grams, so it adds almost nothing to the overall weight of the flash. Sto-Fen are the lightest weight, most effective flash diffuser products on the market today.

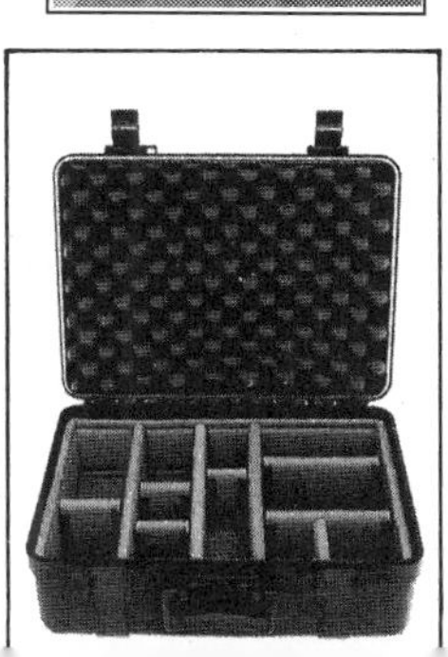

PELI-PELICAN CASES

Watertight and airtight to 30 feet for the ultimate in protection. Constructed of light weight space age structural resin with a neoprene "O" ring seal and exclusive purge valve. Supplied complete with pre-scored pick n'pluck foam or padded dividers. Also includes locking flanges, massive multiple latches for absolute security and best of all, a comfortable molded grip handle.